# THE VIOLENT YEARS

★ ★ ★

## Prohibition and the Detroit Mobs

# THE VIOLENT YEARS

★★★

## Prohibition and the Detroit Mobs

Paul R. Kavieff

BARRICADE
BOOKS

Fort Lee, New Jersey
www.barricadebooks.com

Published by Barricade Books Inc.
185 Bridge Plaza North
Suite 308-A
Fort Lee, NJ 07024

ISBN: 1-56980-210-6

Library of Congress Cataloging-in-Publication Data
Contact the Library of Congress for this information

Printed in the United States of America.

First Printing

# Dedication

I would like to dedicate this book to the loving
memory of my mother, Blanche M. Perlove Kavieff.

# TABLE OF CONTENTS

# Preface

Detroit truly roared in the '20s. The black market opportunities that resulted from national Prohibition created a gold rush atmosphere in the city. Blind pigs, opium dens, gambling, prostitution, and every imaginable form of vice were readily available to the many thousands of manufacturing workers. Banks flush with money legally and illegally made seemed to spring up on every block in the city.

During the mid-'20s, the Purple Gang began to climb to the top of Detroit's underworld pecking order due as much to very good police and city official protection as to their high-profile, strong-arm methods of operation. The city was a breeding ground for violent underworld gangs. By 1925, the survivors of the Giannola/Vitale Mafia wars of 1918-1921 had established themselves as the principal rumrunners on the Detroit River. The River Gang, as it came to be known, controlled most of the large-scale rumrunning north and south of the city. This organization operated a taxi service. Anyone interested in hauling large amounts of liquor across the river contracted with the River Gang, who would then purchase and transport the load. The gang received a percentage of the value of the cargo in return for their service. This early Mafia organization got their money regardless of whether the load had to be dumped or was lost in some way. They essentially operated risk free. Any independents caught running liquor on the river without the okay of the River Gang were killed, their liquor confiscated, and their boats sunk.

Other underworld organizations specialized in all types of mayhem. The Jaworski Gang, working out of Hamtramck (a town within the Detroit city limits), specialized in high-profile bank and payroll robberies. This Mob also worked in Pennsylvania, where they went under the name of the Flathead Gang and spent their time robbing mining company payrolls.

The Carson/Kozak Mob, also working out of Hamtramck, robbed filling stations, local banks, and stuck up pedestrians. Any business or individual was fair game for this predatory band of thugs.

The predominantly Irish "Legs" Laman Gang specialized in kidnapping gangsters and wealthy gamblers. They reasoned that other underworld characters would not go to the police. Their methods were very effective for several years, until they became greedy and began to kidnap and murder legitimate people.

Although national Prohibition ended in December of 1933, the strong criminal/political linkages forged as the result of money made during the Prohibition era continued to protect the underworld. This was especially true for the underworld gambling operators who had developed an organized system of graft payments to Detroit area police and city officials. The enormity of this system was exposed in 1939 and resulted in a grand jury investigation, which all but destroyed organized gambling in Detroit and the surrounding communities. The only underworld outfit to survive the chaos of Prohibition in Detroit was the River Gang, whose leaders became the founders of Detroit's modern Mafia family.

Paul R. Kavieff
Royal Oak, Michigan
July 2001

# Introduction:

## The Origins of the Mafia and the Tradition of Old World Organized Crime

To appreciate the dual roles of benefactor and malefactor that organized crime leaders have always played within their community, it is necessary to understand how this pattern of social relationships evolved. No better example can be found than in 19th-century Sicily. The Sicilian term "Mafia" had originally meant a place of refuge. Later the word was used to describe admirable qualities, such as individualism, beauty, and strength, in a man. The term was not used in reference to crime or criminal brotherhoods until some time after the annexation of Sicily to Italy by popular vote in 1860. After the annexation, the term came into frequent use—especially among northern Italian officials—in reference to the cattle rustling, vendetta feuds, and general lawlessness in certain parts of Sicily.

The Mafia became powerful in Sicily as the result of the abolition of feudalism in the early 19th century. With the disappearance of the centuries-old feudal system, the rural land barons who owned the large country estates became disinterested in the day-to-day operation of their lands. Many took up residence in the cities and leased their land to a new class of entrepreneurs called "gabellotti."

The "gabellotti"—meaning "tax collectors" or "excise men" in Sicilian—paid these landowners a yearly fee and were responsible for the daily operation of the leased estates. Like the barons that had preceded them, they hired a class of armed guards known as "campieri," to protect the estates from bandit gangs and rustlers. These guards were generally recruited from the ranks of the peasants who worked the land on the large estates. Because they had to be familiar with the use of violence, the campieri were often composed of a disproportionate number of men who were outlaws themselves.

Over the years, the gabellotti began using their armed guards for much more than the protection of the property under their charge. The campieri often became a private armed force that was used to keep the peasants who farmed the large country estates in line. They extorted money from local property owners and businessmen, and imposed the will of the local gabellotti, or boss, upon that region's people.

Sometimes the gabellotti would use their armed guards to terrorize the baron from whom they leased the estate. They would threaten his life by shooting in his direction as he traveled through the countryside. The terrified landowner would then run to the gabellotti, who would promise him protection and sometimes suggest to the baron that he put his estate up for auction. When the estate was put on the market, the gabellotti who leased it would conveniently be the only bidder. By the latter part of the 19th century, these methods allowed the gabellotti to consolidate their power in the rural areas of Sicily and become power brokers in their own right.

It was during this time that the gabellotti and their guards began to be referred to as the Mafia.

The peasants who worked the land on the large country estates in Sicily were completely dependent upon the local gabellotti bosses for their livelihood. These Mafia groups became entrenched in the rural areas of Sicily as the local authorities. The peasants often viewed the power of the local Mafia chief to be more legitimate than that of the central Italian-controlled government, which they considered disinterested in local matters—especially when they were the problems of Sicilians.

Eventually the campieri who had once policed the estates took control of the countryside of Sicily and engaged in both legal and illegal occupations with impunity.

After universal suffrage was expanded in Sicily in 1882, the gabellotti's position as local bosses became even more secure as they could then guarantee the local politician of his district's vote. In this way, the local minister could be assured of retaining his seat in the Italian government when election time arrived. In return for bringing in the vote, the local Mafia boss was allowed a free hand in his locality to rule as he saw fit with little to fear from the law-enforcement authorities of the central government.

The authority of rural Mafia groups was further insulated by the Sicilian code of "Omerta." Omerta is often defined as the Mafia code of silence, but in reality it was much more. In Sicily, this form of social behavior had developed over the course of centuries of being ruled and exploited by various foreign powers. The code of Omerta stressed that a man must resolve his own problems without recourse to the authorities. By acting in this manner, a man confirmed his "manliness." The power of the central government was distrusted and held to be illegitimate.

As the result of these complex social relationships, the Sicilian peasants began to rely on the local Mafia boss to provide some of the services that the central government would not furnish. These services included the borrowing of money, help in settling a legal dispute, the rendering of justice on the local level, or help with a personal or legal problem. Although the local Mafia boss could be cruel, he could also be paternalistic. The peasants both feared and admired these local bosses upon whom their lives were so dependent.

In this respect, the old-time Sicilian underworld leader or mafioso brought with him when he immigrated to America an aura of authority among the people in his ethnic community. These men often looked out for the welfare of the immigrant communities upon which they preyed. As European immigrants established close-knit communities in the United States, they maintained their tradition. In the case of Sicilian immigrants, they maintained the code of Omerta, and chose to live and die by the tyranny of local Mafia leaders rather than rely on the help of the local government. But as you read this text, you will notice that virtually all of the crime groups discussed—be it the predominantly Jewish Purple Gang or the predominantly Irish "Legs" Laman Gang—have a strong connection to their ethnic roots and developed their power base within their communities.

# The Giannola/Vitale Gang War

"The directory of Gangland is a complicated affair. Life in that last of the absolute monarchies runs not in straight lines but in sharp zigzags. Leaderships, alliances, friendships and enemies are constantly changing."
—*The Detroit News*, 1923

The modern Detroit area underworld organization was born out of one of the bloodiest gang wars in the history of the underworld. It began shortly after the Michigan Prohibition Law became effective on May 1, 1918. This internecine warfare, which became known as the Giannola/Vitale Gang War, was to rage for nearly three years. Before it ended, all of the established leaders of both of the warring factions would be dead. Antonio (Tony), Sam, and Vito Giannola immigrated to the United States from Sicily around the turn of the century. The three brothers eventually settled in Detroit's Italian community, which was located on the city's lower east side.

During that time, the local Sicilian underworld was dominated by two brothers known as Salvatore and Vito Adamo. The Adamo brothers controlled the rackets in Detroit's Italian community. At first, there was an uneasy alliance between the Giannola and Adamo gangs. This period of cooperation only lasted a short time as the Giannola Mob had their own grand designs on the Adamo-controlled rackets. Once the Giannola brothers became established in the community, the trouble began.

• • •

Both the Adamo and the Giannola groups were involved in the typical ethnic rackets of that era. These underworld enterprises included the Italian lottery, kidnapping for ransom, the peddling of homemade beer and wine, and the "Black Hand" extortion racket.

The origins of the term Black Hand have been traced by some scholars to late 19th century Spain, where it was said to have been the name of an underworld group of thieves and murderers who had styled themselves as protectors of the people. Other research has suggested that the Black Hand may have been a secret society that had fought against the government and the Church in Spain during the Inquisition.

It is important at this point to note that many individual criminals and groups of two or three malefactors practiced the Black Hand form of extortion. These people were often not affiliated with any formal Italian or Sicilian underworld organizations such as the Camorra or the Mafia. For these underworld opportunists, the Black Hand racket was merely a simple means of squeezing money out of their fellow countrymen. This form of extortion was extremely effective on the newly arrived and superstitious Sicilian and Italian immigrants who associated the Black Hand with the secret criminal brotherhoods of their native countries. Once these people arrived in the United States, they were often insulated in their own communities, unfamiliar with the culture and customs of their newly adopted country, and distrustful of established institutions of authority. Many of these immigrants felt helpless and terrified when they received a Black Hand letter. Those who were unfortunate enough to be sent such correspondence believed it to be the work of an all-powerful underworld organization known as the Black Hand, from which there was no escape.

All that the Black Hand extortion technique required was the writing of a threatening letter— often illustrated with crude drawings of daggers dripping with blood, a black handprint, a knife-pierced heart, a gun firing, or a bomb exploding. The letter would sometimes contain a subtle threat cloaked in flowery language. At other times, the letter would come blatantly to the point, threatening the victim with immediate death or the death of a family member if the extortion demands were not met. Often a Black Hand letter might suggest that the victim seek out an intermediary who could negotiate with the mysterious Black Hand. This intermediary would often be easier to find than the victim imagined, because in reality it would sometimes be the author of the Black Hand letter.

The usual consequences of ignoring a Black Hand threat would be the destruction of the victim's place of business or home by bombing or arson, the murder or kidnapping of a family member, or the murder of the victim himself.

• • •

As was tradition, the immigrant Italian and Sicilian community of the early 20th century often developed a love/hate relationship with the local underworld leaders. The Giannola brothers were known in their community as the "Triumvirate of

Terror," yet they also served at times in the role of community benefactors. Tony Giannola was known to have helped the aged and the poor in his community, sometimes providing free coal in the winter when people could not afford to buy fuel, or food on the table when a family was destitute and had nothing to eat. Some residents in Giannola's community even claimed that Tony had actually done more to stop the Black Hand from operating than the Detroit Police Department.

For several years, the streets of Detroit's lower east side were the scene of open warfare between the Giannola and Adamo factions. Bodies were often found blown to pieces with shotguns or with their throats cut. The sawed-off shotgun became the weapon of choice among the feuding gangs. As the gang war dragged on, men on both sides died violent deaths.

Tony Giannola was often arrested and questioned by the police during the gang war, but officials could never get enough evidence against him to hold him on a specific charge. Tony was considered by the Detroit police to be the brains behind the Giannola Mob and the man responsible for most of the crime in the Italian community. According to Detroit Police Inspector William Good, chief of the Sicilian Squad, whenever "Tony Giannola was brought in for questioning he would shrug his shoulders, roll his eyes and look at the ceiling. He always had an alibi."

Tony Giannola was convicted of a crime only once, and that was careless use of firearms. It seems that Tony and several of his henchmen had been riding down a Detroit street when they passed two pedestrians who had the misfortune of resembling

Vito and Salvatore Adamo. Both of these men were immediately shot to death. Shortly after the shooting incident, Giannola's auto was stopped by a patrol car. The officers found two empty sawed-off shotguns and an empty revolver in the car. All of the weapons had been recently fired. Unfortunately, what police couldn't find were witnesses that would be willing to testify against these men. The end result of Giannola's conviction was the payment of a $200 fine.

Many say the final incident in the Giannola/Adamo war occurred when Ferdinand Palma, a local banker and a personal friend of Tony Giannola, received a Black Hand letter. The letter had been authored by one of the Adamo brothers. Tony Giannola intervened in the extortion plot and warned the Adamo Mob to lay off his friend. Palma, in the belief that he was protected, ignored the demands of the letter and shortly afterward was shot and seriously wounded.

The war with the Adamo brothers finally ended when the two men were caught walking along Mullet Street near Russell and shot down by Giannola assassins.

The deaths of the Adamo brothers left the Giannola Mob in complete control of the Italian/Sicilian underworld, both in Detroit and in the downriver communities of Ecorse and Wyandotte. The Giannola organization at this time was composed of about 50 men. The Giannola brothers established the Wyandotte Fruit Co. and several other legitimate businesses, and for a while they prospered.

When Prohibition arrived in Michigan in 1918, the Giannola Mob was well established. The Giannola brothers quickly grasped the opportunities created by the new Prohibition Law and became involved in rum-running and hijacking.

Soon after the Michigan statewide Prohibition Law went into effect, U.S. 25, known as Dixie Highway, became a popular route for rumrunners bringing liquor to Detroit from Toledo, Ohio, and other areas. This roughly 60-mile link of road between Detroit and Toledo would become popularly referred to as the "Rumrunners Runway" and the "Avenue De Booze." The Giannola gang made a profitable business out of hijacking trucks and autos bringing contraband liquor into Michigan along U.S. 25. They also began working the lower Detroit River, hijacking liquor as it was being moved from boats to trucks by small gangs of rumrunners and independents. It wasn't long before the Giannola brothers began to purchase boats and establish themselves as rumrunners, buying their liquor in Canada and hauling it across the Detroit River to points in Wyandotte and Ecorse.

Shortly after the Adamo brothers were murdered, Sam Cipriano, a Giannola underboss and partner in their beer business, received a package in the mail. He took the box over to a friend who owned a nearby drugstore. When the two men opened the box, it exploded in their faces. The gift-wrapped bomb detonated with such force that it blew out the front of the drugstore, instantly killing the druggist and ripping off one of Cipriano's arms. Cipriano managed to stagger into St. Mary's Hospital, where he died several hours later.

Around the same time, another Giannola lieutenant, John Vitale, was being investigated by detectives of the Detroit Police Department's Sicilian

Squad. They suspected that he was one of a group of men who had set up and ambushed Detective Sergeant Emmanuel Roggers, who was shot to death on July 24, 1917. Roggers had been a member of the Sicilian Squad. Police theorized that Roggers, who was investigating the Giannola brothers, had found out too much and for this reason had been eliminated. However, in early 1918, John Vitale broke from the Giannola Mob and set out with a gang of his own. This group was for the most part composed of former Giannola gangsters.

The actual reason for the trouble between the Giannola brothers and John Vitale, which resulted in the split of the Vitale faction from the Giannola Mob, is not known for certain. As a partner in the Giannola beer business, John Vitale had been allowed to run his own crew semi-independently of the Giannola gang, although he still was required to account to the Giannola brothers for his activities. It is possible that Vitale had grown tired of working for the Giannola brothers. Vitale could see the fabulous profits that could be made in rum-running and other Prohibition-related ventures and did not want to share the spoils with the Giannola brothers.

Another theory behind the Giannola/Vitale split involves Peter Bosco, a close friend of John Vitale's and a fellow Giannola gangster who had been involved in a business deal with Tony Giannola. Bosco had been part-owner of a grocery store with Tony Giannola in Detroit. Apparently Giannola thought that Bosco was taking more than his fair share of the profits out of the business. The business arrangement ended in a dispute between the two men, and they parted company. Shortly after Peter Bosco and Tony Giannola had dissolved their partnership, Bosco opened up a garage in Detroit. At first, the Giannolas' men attempted to kill Bosco by rigging his auto to explode upon starting by filling the cylinders with gasoline. When police investigators attempted to move the vehicle, it blew up. Several Detroit police officers involved in the investigation barely escaped injury when the car exploded. Then one night Bosco was ambushed and shot to death in his garage. John Vitale at this point swore revenge for the murder of his friend, and the Vitale faction broke from the Giannola Mob.

The Giannola and Vitale Mobs had coexisted in relative peace for a time but—as could be expected—business competition and personal rivalries led to killings and reprisals for killings, which ultimately pushed the two Mobs to an all-out war.

The incident that triggered the war occurred in November of 1918. John Vitale arranged a business deal with Canadian suppliers to have 41 barrels of whiskey sent to Detroit via the Wabash Railroad in a freight car marked as fruit. This liquor shipment was valued at $13,000. Vitale thought that labeling the contraband-loaded freight car as a fruit shipment consigned to him would provide a good cover, as both he and Giannola were legitimate fruit dealers.

Somehow the Giannola gang learned about Vitale's liquor shipment. They located the freight car in a railway yard, arrived with trucks, broke open the seals on the freight-car doors, and stole the whiskey. They liked Vitale's cover so much themselves that after they had loaded the whiskey into their trucks they covered the load with green peppers and other produce.

Unknown to either the Giannola or Vitale gangs, the Detroit police had been tipped off about the

freight car and staked out the railroad yards waiting for somebody to show up with trucks and pick up
the load. Police followed the liquor-loaded Giannola
trucks back to Wyandotte, arrested most of the
gang, including the Giannola brothers, and confiscated the liquor. When John Vitale learned of this
incident, he supposedly became enraged and swore
revenge on the Giannola brothers. It was this incident that in all likelihood precipitated the Giannola/
Vitale Gang War.

Tony Giannola became the first casualty of the
war. On January 3, 1919, Tony was driven by his
bodyguard, Tony Alescio, to attend the wake of a
close friend named Giuseppe Braziola. Braziola had
been shot to death by his son-in-law in a family
argument. As Tony Giannola stepped from his car to
attend the gathering, Alescio pulled his automatic
pistol and fired five rapid shots. Tony Giannola
plunged forward and collapsed, a bullet in his brain
and four more slugs in his back. Tony Alescio,
Giannola's bodyguard, had been adopted and raised
by the Giannola family since childhood. No one ever
suspected that he was a Vitale spy.

At the time that Tony Giannola was murdered,
he was waiting to stand trial in federal court. He
had been indicted by the feds for violation of the Car
Seal Act in the freight yard whiskey theft. If found
guilty, Giannola could have received up to 10 years
in prison. Tony Giannola's funeral became one of the
first extravagant gangster funerals in Detroit.
Within a month, an attempt would be made on the
life of Sam Giannola by the Vitale Mob.

On the evening of February 2, 1919, Sam
Giannola and his brother-in-law, Pasquale Danni,
had just arrived at Sam's Ford City, Michigan, home.

As Giannola and Danni walked up to the house, assassins hiding in the bushes opened fire. Danni was killed instantly in the shotgun attack, but Sam Giannola managed to escape the ambush unharmed.

Giannola was quick to retaliate for the murder of his brother-in-law. On the morning of February 5, 1919, John Vitale's store in Ford City was shot up by a group of gunmen who drove by the building, but no one was hurt in the attack.

That same night Sheriff Coffin led a force of Wayne County deputies and detectives into Ford City to arrest John Vitale and, hopefully, solve the Tony Giannola and Pasquale Danni murders. As the detachment of police pulled up to Vitale's store, a group of men that had been standing outside the building opened fire on the lawmen, wounding one of the officers in the leg. Ten men, including John Vitale, were arrested in the raid. Vitale was later booked for the murder of Pasquale Danni and locked up in the Wayne County Jail.

On February 28, 1919, Vito Renda and Sam Evola, both Vitale lieutenants, went to the Wayne County Jail to visit John Vitale. On their way to the jail, they had met Joe Vitale, John's 17-year-old son, who decided to accompany the two men on the visit.

The Giannola gang had received information that Renda and Evola would be coming to the Wayne County Jail to confer with the boss. Sam Giannola and three of his gunmen went to the jail. Two men waited outside of the building in an automobile with the motor running. The two other gunmen went into the Wayne County Jail and waited patiently in the corridors for John Vitale's visitors to arrive. A deputy at the Wayne County Jail named

Philip Jasnewski later told Detroit police that he had noticed two men loitering in the corridor of the jail shortly before noon. The corridor of the old Wayne County Jail fronts Raynor Street and separated the jail entrance from the property room and cell block area. When Jasnewski inquired of the two men what their business was they said, "Oh, we're just waiting for some Italian fellows." Moments later, one of the deputies in a room across the corridor opened the heavy steel door to let Jasnewski know that his lunch was ready. According to the statement later made by Deputy Jasnewski, he had gotten halfway across the corridor when three men walked into the Raynor Street entrance of the jail. As they entered, the two men who had been waiting in the corridor stepped out of the shadows and said hello to Renda. Renda acknowledged the greeting. As Evola pushed the cell block door buzzer to be admitted, the two men pulled pistols and opened fire on the three visitors. Although police would later discover that Renda, Evola, and Vitale were all armed, they never had a chance to use their weapons to defend themselves. Jasnewski, who was unarmed, dove for cover when the shooting started. The two gunmen emptied their pistols, mostly at Renda, and fled out the Raynor Street door of the Wayne County Jail.

Deputy William Parmenter, who had opened the door to the cell block after Evola had rung, dragged Evola and young Vitale into the cell block area, probably saving their lives. Parmenter would later describe the sound of the bullets ricocheting off the cell block door as if someone were trying to effect a jail break by hitting the door with a heavy hammer.

Another man named E.M. Steffe, supposedly the

only eyewitness to the shooting incident through its entire duration, had been waiting in the lobby of the Wayne County Jail. Steffe claimed that when the two assassins saw Evola, Renda, and Vitale enter the jail, they stepped up to shake hands with one of the three men, and one of the two yelled, "These are the birds—shoot."

At approximately the same time that the shootings were taking place inside the Wayne County Jail, Sergeant Forrest Hull and Patrolman Al Transke of the Highland Park Police Department pulled up to the curb in front of the jail in a squad car. As they stopped the vehicle, they could hear the last shots being fired inside the jail. They watched as the two gunmen burst out of the Raynor Street entrance of the jail and ran up the street toward a black Studebaker sedan. There the two accomplices waited in the getaway car that was parked a short distance up the street. Transke yelled for the gunmen to halt and then opened fire on them. As Transke ran after them, he emptied his pistol. Transke later claimed that he thought one of the gunmen may have been hit by his fire, as the man stumbled and fell just as he reached the vehicle. The other men lifted the wounded man into the car, as it screeched off at a high rate of speed, turning onto Gratiot Avenue. Hull and Transke attempted to pursue the gunmen but lost sight of their car upon reaching the next block.

Vito Renda had been shot 20 times and was mortally wounded. Evola had been hit 12 times, and Joe Vitale had been shot through the abdomen and was not expected to live. Both gunmen carried two pistols each.

All three of the wounded men refused to give

police any information about their assailants. They also refused to talk to Assistant Wayne County Prosecutor Harry Keidan. Renda, however, told Keidan that he would talk with Recorders Court Judge Charles Wilkins, whose court was in session at the time of the shooting incident. Judge Wilkins adjourned the case he was hearing to go to Renda's bedside. Renda told Wilkins that he had recognized one of his assailants as Sam Giannola. He also identified the other gunman. Later the same day, Joe Vitale would also name Giannola as one of the gunmen but refused to identify the other man.

Realizing that death was imminent, Renda seemed to be in a mood to confess. He requested to speak with Wilkins specifically to inform him that Tony and Sam Giannola had, at one time, plotted to kill him. According to Renda, the reason that the Giannola brothers wanted to eliminate the judge was because Wilkins had given a stiff prison sentence to an auto thief who had been a close friend of theirs and a member of the Giannola Mob.

Shortly after identifying Sam Giannola as one of the assassins, Vito Renda died. Neither the two gunmen nor their confederates in the getaway car were ever brought to trial. Sam Giannola was arrested for the murder of Vito Renda, but Giannola was able to produce witnesses who swore that he had been in the Chamber of Commerce Building located at State and Griswold Streets during the time that the shootings had taken place. Giannola was held without bail for a short time and released for lack of evidence.

The Giannola/Vitale Gang War continued to rage through 1919. Finally, a tentative truce was arranged between the two gangs that fall. Sam Giannola, who had grown weary from almost two years of hostilities, put his faith in the agreement and began going around in public without his bodyguards. On October 2, 1919, he was shot down by three gunmen in front of a crowd of horrified onlookers as he walked out of a bank located at the corner of Russell and Monroe Streets.

After the murder of Sam Giannola, John Vitale dropped out of sight. Leaders in the Giannola Mob decided that to kill John Vitale they would have to bring in an assassin from out of state, someone that nobody in the Vitale Gang would be able to recognize. A gunman named Angelo (Angel Face) Torres was brought in from New York to do the deed.

Sam Russo, a Vitale gangster and reputedly one of the men responsible for the murder of Sam Giannola, was the first gang warfare death of 1920. His body was found at the junction of Miller and Cabot Roads. Russo had been stabbed and shot to death.

Tony Alescio, the slayer of Tony Giannola and his erstwhile bodyguard, was shot to death on January 28, 1920. Five other Vitale gangsters were murdered in rapid succession. Torres had evidently been busy, but he had not succeeded in cornering John Vitale.

On August 17, 1920, at approximately 6:05 a.m., John Vitale and his son Joe were ambushed in front of their home on Russell Street in Detroit, as they were climbing into their car. The shots were fired from a second-story window in a house directly across the street from the Vitale home. The assassins opened fire on Vitale and his son with shotguns. Vitale's son Joe, the same man who had been severely wounded in the Wayne County Jail shooting incident, was killed instantly in the barrage. At the first sound of gunfire, Vitale's wife had run screaming out of the house and attempted to drag the body of her dead son to cover. John Vitale instinctively ducked behind the auto and was only slightly wounded in the hand.

As the killers fled from the scene of the attack, some of the people in the neighborhood attempted to chase after them but were scared off when the gunmen stopped and fired several shots in their direction. The four triggermen ran to the home of a Mrs. Louis Burke several blocks away and asked if they could use her telephone to call a cab. They waited in the kitchen of the Burke home at least a half hour, until a taxi arrived and took them downtown. This all occurred during the time that the Detroit police had been scouring the neighborhood looking for the killers. Detectives later found four shotguns at and near the vicinity in which the shootings occurred.

During the Detroit Police Department's investigation of the murder, detectives would discover that the killers had rented a room across the street from the Vitale home on July 21, 1920, and had been patiently waiting for their opportunity.

Seven men were later arrested as suspects in the case, but the witnesses, who included both Mrs. Burke and the cab driver, failed to make a positive identification. It was rumored in the Detroit underworld that the men who had killed John Vitale's son in the botched assassination attempt had returned to Buffalo, New York, shortly after the attack. They had been brought to Detroit by the Giannola old guard for the sole purpose of slaying John Vitale.

Joe Vitale was the oldest of John's two sons. At the time of his death, he had been awaiting trial on a charge of carrying concealed weapons. About five weeks before he was murdered, he had pulled a pistol and fired several shots when a Detroit police officer had tried to search him.

At approximately 3 a.m. on September 28, 1920, the long vendetta finally caught up with John Vitale. He was on his way to the Michigan Central Station, when his driver slowed the car and pulled to a stop at the curb. The driver leaned out of the window and said that he thought that one of the tires was going flat. Suddenly the door flew open, and Vitale was pushed out of the car and made a target for gunmen who had been waiting in the dark. The killers instantly opened fire with sawed-off shotguns. Vitale's legs, shoulders, chest, and head were perforated with buckshot before his lifeless body hit the ground. Witnesses to the shooting claimed that they saw two vehicles pull away from the scene of the murder, but they could not see the faces of any of the men involved.

Many believe that Vitale's murder was set up by his own men. His killers had been waiting for him to be driven to the rendezvous point at 241 14th Street in Detroit. According to underworld rumor, it was his own associates that had coaxed him into going to the Michigan Central Station to meet someone to consummate a liquor deal. The theory that John Vitale had been killed by his own Mob was further supported by the fact that his loaded .32 caliber automatic pistol, complete with extra clip, was found in his pocket. He never pulled it because he never suspected a thing. Vitale was approximately 48 years old at the time of his death.

The Giannola/Vitale Gang War ended in late 1920. All of the leaders of both factions had been killed. The final peace agreement was presided over by Sam Catalonotte. Catalonotte was an elder statesman in the Detroit underworld and was mutually respected by all of the competing underworld factions. Part of the peace agreement he worked out was to divide up the Detroit metropolitan area into districts that could be assigned to the various factions of the Giannola and Vitale gangsters. Each group could then operate their rackets within their own sphere of influence without interference from outsiders. It was believed that this would eliminate feuding and promote cooperation between the various groups.

As long as Catalonotte was alive to mediate disputes, there was relative peace in the Italian community. Catalonotte's death in 1930 touched off another war between the Sicilian and Italian Mobs. The results of this gang war laid the foundation for the present-day Detroit area Mafia or La Cosa Nostra organization.

The various younger men who made up the muscle of the surviving Giannola and Vitale Mobs would eventually form the underworld organization that succeeded the Purple Gang in control of the Detroit underworld. The Giannola/Vitale Gang War broke up the two most powerful Italian underworld organizations in the Detroit area into a number of splinter groups. One of the more powerful and successful of these Mafia gangs was an outfit that came to be known as the River Gang, and they would eventually control all of the rum-running operations on the upper Detroit River.

# The River Gang

"They find a guy stiff on Belle Isle the cops said Pete Licavoli did it. A kidnapping Mob gets going in Detroit. They said Pete Licavoli's a kidnapper. No matter what happens it's either my brother 'Yonnie' [Thomas Licavoli] or myself."

"I never did nothing, I am just a whiskey hauler that's all. I get rapped for that Belle Isle killing because I was working around there. Now I'm broke. You can't pull whiskey with everyone looking for you."

*—Pete Licavoli, 1931*

When the bloody Giannola/Vitale Gang War ended in early 1921, the remnants of both groups formed into a number of independent gangs. Each one of these underworld factions was given the right to operate within its own geographic area in the Detroit region. The disputes that would often arise between the various competing groups were arbitrated and resolved by a small council composed of the most widely respected leaders of the local Sicilian underworld. This leadership body was presided over by Samuel Catalanotte, an underworld diplomat of considerable charisma and ability. Catalanotte promoted the peaceful resolution of disputes, which allowed the various underworld groups to devote their attention to working their rackets. Most of the moneymaking operations had been seriously neglected during the long Giannola/Vitale Gang War.

In the first years of national Prohibition, most of the rum-running business on the Detroit River was conducted by small, independent groups of whiskey haulers. This situation rapidly changed during the early '20s, as the reorganized factions of the old Giannola and Vitale Mobs and other organized Detroit area underworld groups moved to gain control over the liquor and beer traffic from Canada.

The lengthy war between the Giannola and Vitale Mobs seriously depleted the number of gunmen within the ranks of both gangs. Over a period of approximately 10 years, more than 100 men were killed as a result of the strife. Peter and Thomas Licavoli arrived in Detroit from their native St. Louis, Missouri, during this time when new recruits were desperately needed by the various criminal groups.

• • •

The Licavoli brothers were born and raised in St. Louis, Missouri. Their mother and father had immigrated to the United States from Terrasina, Sicily, during the early years of the 20th century. The family eventually settled in a large, red-brick tenement house that was located in a predominately Jewish slum neighborhood in St. Louis. The building reportedly contained 11 three-room flats and housed two stores. One flat, which was located across the hall from where the Licavoli family lived, was used as a Jewish synagogue. The building was eventually purchased by Mathew Licavoli, the boys' father.

It was into this environment that Peter Joseph

Licavoli Sr. was born in 1903, and Thomas Licavoli in 1904. Peter and Thomas were the two oldest children of Mathew Licavoli, whose family would eventually grow to include a younger brother named Dominic and several sisters. Mathew Licavoli and his wife were hardworking, religious people who had dreams of seeing their oldest son Peter become a doctor and Thomas a priest. Time, fate, and the environment in which the boys were to grow up would lead them down a different path. As youngsters, Peter and Thomas sometimes made their spending money running errands for local gangsters. Sometimes during the long summers, they would dive for coins thrown by tourists from passing boats on the Mississippi River. As a result of their neighborhood exposure to the Jewish culture, both boys were reportedly fluent in the Yiddish language.

The Licavoli brothers grew up in a tough section of St. Louis, where the boys began associating with a group of juvenile thugs known as the "Hammerhead Gang." Their colorful name was derived from their method of hitting their victims over the head and knocking them unconscious before robbing them. For several years during the late teens, this juvenile street gang terrorized St. Louis.

Both James Licavoli and Pete Licavoli, cousins of Peter Joseph and Thomas Licavoli, were also members of this early St. Louis street gang. Like his cousins, James Licavoli, who was better known by his underworld alias "Jack White," would settle in Detroit during the early '20s. Once in Detroit, he would find employment as a gunman for the River Gang. In later years, James "Jack White" Licavoli would become an important Mob boss in the Cleveland, Ohio, area. Pete Licavoli, known in the Detroit underworld as "Horseface Pete" and "St.

Louis Pete" to distinguish him from his more famous cousin, would eventually settle in Detroit as well. Horseface Pete would later be convicted of first-degree murder in Detroit Recorders Court for the slaying of a minor Detroit gangster named Henry Tupancy during the Mob wars in the bloody summer of 1930. Horseface Pete died in a Michigan prison.

• • •

Although there is no official record of when Peter Joseph Licavoli Sr. arrived in Detroit, it was probably sometime in 1922. Horseface Pete is often assumed to have settled in Detroit much later, as he successfully managed to avoid being arrested by the Detroit police until 1927. It is believed that Peter Licavoli, who sometimes went by the aliases of "Pete Moceri," "George Rigley," and "Black Pete," was imported to Detroit to work as a gunman for Joseph Moceri, the leader of one of the more powerful splinter groups that had evolved in the aftermath of the Giannola/Vitale Gang War. Eventually Peter ran up a long list of Detroit arrests that would include violation of the Prohibition law, armed robbery, kidnapping and murder.

In 1922, a report to the St. Louis, Missouri, juvenile court described 17-year-old Thomas "Yonnie" Licavoli as "incorrigible." In early 1923, Thomas Licavoli fled St. Louis to avoid prosecution on a concealed weapons charge. He joined the U.S. Navy that same year and promptly deserted, returning home to St. Louis. He was granted amnesty after his desertion from the navy by no less a personage than President Warren G. Harding, shortly before Harding died in office. This act on the part of the President of the United States would seem to indicate that the Licavoli brothers had already developed very good political connections.

In late 1923 or early 1924, Yonnie began working with Francesco "Frank" Cammarata, who was born in Sicily on March 16, 1898. He immigrated to the United States in 1913, arriving in New York and later settling in St. Louis, Missouri. Cammarata was active in the St. Louis underworld for no more than five or six years before moving to Detroit around 1920. He probably began a long association with the Licavoli brothers in the "Hammerhead Gang" of St. Louis and would eventually marry the Licavolis' sister Grace. Once Cammarata settled in the Detroit area, he worked as a hired gunman and bank robber before joining forces with the River Gang in the mid-'20s. After relocating to Detroit and before joining forces with the River Gang, Cammarata and Yonnie Licavoli became partners in the bank robbing and hijacking rackets.

Thomas "Yonnie" Licavoli was always the more aggressive of the two Licavoli brothers. He soon earned a reputation in the Detroit underworld as a ruthless hijacker and strong-arm man. It would be Yonnie Licavoli who would be instrumental in organizing the Moceri/Licavoli River Gang into a force to be reckoned with on the upper Detroit River.

Aside from his rum-running and hijacking activities, Yonnie was interested in several underground saloons, known as blind pigs, and other underworld resorts in the Detroit area. Alvin C. Hoyle and another unidentified man were partners with Yonnie in the ownership of a popular Detroit blind pig known as the Subway Cafe. The Subway Cafe was located in the basement of a building in downtown Detroit. The cafe had been raided and closed several times by Detroit police for gambling and Prohibition law violations. Finally, the owner of the building in which the cafe was operated notified Hoyle and his partners that they would have to move. Licavoli had evidently told Hoyle to wait until they could get together and decide upon an equitable division of the equipment in the cafe, before moving it out. For some reason, Licavoli decided that he was being double crossed by Hoyle, believing that he was taking jointly owned property out of the blind pig without his okay. In an effort to set up Hoyle, Yonnie made arrangements with him to assist in moving the remaining equipment out of the Subway Cafe one night in the late summer of 1926. A young man names Charles Phillips, who had worked at the Subway as a bouncer, was hired by Hoyle to help the men move their equipment. According to testimony that was later given to the Detroit police by Phillips, Hoyle said that Licavoli called and told him that he had arranged to borrow a truck which the men could use to move the equipment. Hoyle asked Phillips to come along and drive the truck for them. On the night they had planned to move the equipment, Licavoli came by in a car and picked up Hoyle and Phillips. According to Phillips, Hoyle got into the front seat with Licavoli, and Phillips sat in the back seat next to a man who had accompanied Licavoli. Phillips told police that he had never seen this man before. The four men drove to a dark street on Detroit's east side near the Elmwood Cemetery. Licavoli pointed to a dark driveway where he told the men that they could find the truck. As the four men walked up the driveway, the shooting began. Hoyle was killed instantly. Phillips was shot 14 times but somehow managed to survive. He described to police how a gunman had stood over him as he lay writhing from pain on the ground from wounds he had received only moments before. The gunman emptied his pistol into Phillips's hat. The killer's poor aim was the only reason why Phillips was still alive. There were five furrows in Phillips's scalp and five bullet holes in his straw hat. Of the other nine wounds, none was deeper than a flesh wound. Yonnie Licavoli was not wounded and denied that he had been with Hoyle and Phillips the night they were shot. Licavoli was briefly held as a suspect in Hoyle's murder. Phillips, who had identified Licavoli from his hospital bed, disappeared after recovering from his wounds, and the case was dropped.

• • •

When Frank Cammarata was not working with the River Gang, he sometimes supplemented his income by robbing banks in the Detroit area. On the morning of July 1, 1925, four gunmen patiently waited outside the People's Bank of Wayne County located at the corner of Grand River and Brooklyn Avenues in Detroit. The men were waiting for the bank's bookkeeper to arrive that morning. When the bookkeeper walked up to the bank, the four men pushed him inside as he opened the front door. At gunpoint, they forced the terrified man to open the safe from which they took $2,100 in silver coins and escaped. Cammarata was the only one of the bandits that was positively identified by witnesses as participating in the holdup. On September 22, 1925, he was arrested by Detroit police and arraigned in Detroit Recorders Court on charges of armed robbery. He was released on a bond of $10,000 to await trial on the charge.

On November 7, 1925, five gunmen armed with sawed-off shotguns and pistols held up the Kleiner Cigar Manufacturing Company in Detroit. Patrolman Edward Gerdes, with only two weeks on the police force, had been assigned from the Chene

Street station to guard the company's payroll. Gerdes accompanied Stanley Rootes, who was the Kleiner Company paymaster, to the Central Savings Bank at Chene Street and Harper Avenue. When the two men returned with the payroll to the Kleiner Plant, they were assaulted by five gunmen who jumped out of a parked car and began firing wildly. Rootes dropped the payroll bag, which contained between $8,700 and $10,000, and threw up his hands. Gerdes, who was wounded in the legs, managed to use his own shotgun before he fell and wounded one of the bandits. The five men grabbed the payroll bag and escaped, taking their wounded comrade with them. Cammarata was identified by witnesses who had watched the gunfight as one of the five men who held up the Kleiner Company. Gerdes identified Cammarata as the man he saw come towards him with a pistol in his hand after Gerdes had been wounded.

Cammarata, who was still out on bond and awaiting trial on the People's Bank of Wayne County robbery charge, was arrested again on November 11, 1925, and charged with the Kleiner holdup. After a second arraignment in less than two months in Recorders Court on a charge of armed robbery, Cammarata furnished the new bond of $20,000 and promptly disappeared. On November 18, 1925, his $20,000 bond was forfeited because of his failure to appear in Court. Cammarata returned to St. Louis, where he was arrested on January 2, 1926.

The Detroit police theorized that the Kleiner robbery was an inside job. The bandits' car pulled up at the same time that Gerdes and Rootes had returned with the company payroll. The gunmen's abandoned car was later found by Detroit police with five sawed-off shotguns inside. Detectives believed that one of the bandits' girlfriends might have been an employee at the Kleiner Company and had tipped the gang off as to the time that the payroll usually arrived.

The first Kleiner holdup trial was declared a mistrial by Recorders Court Judge W. McKay Skillman after a woman who had been a spectator at the trial was discovered to have told jurors during a lunch break that Frank Cammarata was innocent. The woman, a Mrs. Catherine Ivy, was lectured by Judge Skillman and then sentenced to 30 days in the Detroit House of Corrections for contempt of court.

At Cammarata's second trial in the Kleiner robbery case, several witnesses appeared on behalf of the defense and stated that Cammarata had not been identified by Gerdes when the police officer had viewed him from his hospital bed. Cammarata's girlfriend claimed that he had been with her during the day and time of the Kleiner holdup. Cammarata stated that he had dropped his girlfriend off at work on the day in question and returned to his apartment, where he slept most of the day. When cross-examined by Assistant Wayne County Prosecutor James Chenot, Cammarata could not remember the address of his apartment or where he had borrowed the Pierce-Arrow car that he was driving when he was arrested. Gerdes, the Detroit police officer who was wounded in the holdup, was the only witness to positively identify Cammarata. Several weeks after the robbery of the Kleiner Cigar Manufacturing Company, Gerdes was mysteriously shot by unknown gunmen while on duty. He believed that he had been shot by friends of Cammarata to keep him from testifying at the trial. Stanley Rootes, the auditor and paymaster at the Kleiner Cigar Manufacturing Company who had been carrying the payroll bag at the time of the holdup, failed to identify Frank Cammarata as one of the bandits.

Cammarata's second trial in the Kleiner robbery case was again declared a mistrial after the jury had deliberated more than 24 hours and were released by Judge W. Skillman McKay. Cammarata was eventually acquitted in the Kleiner Cigar Company holdup. He was still awaiting trail on the People's Bank of Wayne County robbery charge, when he and Thomas Licavoli were arrested in Canada on a concealed weapons charge.

There is some evidence that Frank Cammarata, Pete Corrado (later an important leader in the Detroit Mob), and Thomas Licavoli may have been operating a stolen-car ring out of Detroit during the mid-'20s. On June 12, 1925, they were indicted by a Federal Grand Jury on a charge of violation of the Federal Dyer Act (driving a stolen car across state lines). The feds had found proof in shipping records that they were investigating at that time that Cammarata, Licavoli, and Corrado had shipped at least three stolen cars to Buffalo, New York, by boat. Once the vehicles had arrived in Buffalo, they had obtained New York plates for the cars and then driven them back to Detroit for resale. The three men never went to trial on the charge, as other events had begun to shape their futures.

Aside from their other rackets, both Frank Cammarata and Yonnie Licavoli were important leaders in the River Gang. Their partners in this venture were Joe Moceri, Pete Licavoli, and Joe Massei. Joe Massei was a downriver bootlegger, rumrunner, and gunman. Massei was a highly respected, well-liked leader in the Detroit underworld. The son of an Italian father and Irish mother, Massei was to eventually become an important national underworld figure.

By ruthless methods, the River Gang consolidated their control over most of the large-scale rum-running activities on the upper Detroit River between the eastern city limits of Detroit and Mt. Clemens, Michigan. According to one Detroit underworld source, the River Gang operated outside of the Detroit city limits to make it more difficult for the Detroit police to interfere in their activities. According to another account, most of the newly arrived gangsters in the Detroit area stayed out of the city because by the mid-'20s, the Purple Gang and its various factions maintained a tight control over the Detroit underworld's most lucrative rackets.

The River Gang never hauled its own loads. The gang made its money by carrying the loads of other rumrunners in its boats and charging a 25 percent tax for protection on whatever the load of liquor was worth on the retail market. If their speedboats were pursued by the U.S. Coast Guard or Customs' cutters and the loads had to be dumped into the Detroit River it was the owner's loss and not the River Gang's. Any whiskey haulers who refused to use the services of the River Gang and attempted to run their own loads were frequently hijacked, beaten, or worse. If they continued to haul liquor without paying tribute to the River Gang, they would often disappear. The hijacking of independent rumrunners occurred so frequently that by the later '20s most of the larger independents were either paying protection money to the River Gang or had been forced out of business.

Pete Licavoli's consent counted as much as the government's if you wanted to run liquor as an independent whiskey hauler on the Detroit River. According to one account, "it was not wise to go into business without Pete Licavoli's okay, as your first trip may be your last."

A number of men who were associated with the River Gang during the period 1925-1930 would become important leaders in the modern-day Detroit area Mafia organization. Among those who worked in various capacities for the River Gang during this period were: Sam Orlando, Tony Orlando, James Moceri, Mike Moceri, Vito Scola, Joe Marlow, Moses Massu, Joe Mercurio, Tom Delano, Angelo Meli, James Pizimenti, Mike Rubino, Barilow Frontiera, Art Simmons, Gerald Lewis, Dominic Badalamenti, Charles Aiello, Sam Palazzola, Frank La Rosa, William Steinberg, Martin Thomas, Mel Raymon, Burt Medica, Mat Species, Tony Parisi, Elmer Macklin, James Licavoli, Sam Paul, John Ventimeglia, and Joe Tallman.

On September 8, 1927, an event would occur that would have important consequences on the evolution of not only the River Gang, but also the future underworld organizations of both Detroit and Toledo, Ohio. Acting on an anonymous telephone tip, members of the Windsor Police and the Ontario Provincial Police busted into a room in Windsor's Prince Edward Hotel and arrested Thomas Licavoli and Frank Cammarata. The men were reported by the Windsor, Ontario, police to be suspects in the $15,000 robbery of a liquor export dock in LaSalle, Ontario, the previous week. In reality, the anonymous telephone caller had told the Windsor Police that the two men were registered at the hotel and that they had pistols in their possession. Exactly what Licavoli and Cammarata were doing in Windsor at that time is open to speculation. One rumor that was circulating in the Detroit under-world was that the two men had gone to Windsor to kidnap some wealthy liquor exporters. A loaded U.S. Army .45 caliber automatic pistol was found in their room, tucked under the pillow on "Yonnie" Licavoli's bed. A .38 caliber automatic pistol was also found in the side pocket of Cammarata's car, which was parked in the hotel's garage. Both men were arrested and charged with having "offensive weapons" in their possession in Canada without a permit. They were held at the Essex County Jail in Sandwich, Ontario, pending their arraignment on the charge.

Both Licavoli and Cammarata were granted bail bonds of $15,000 each, which they were unable to raise. At their trial in the Essex, Ontario, Court House in October 1927, defense attorneys for the two men argued that the two guns that had been found by the police actually belonged to two other men whom Licavoli and Cammarata knew only by their first names as Tony and Joe. Tony and Joe were supposedly hired by Licavoli and Cammarata to run liquor across the river to Detroit for them. The jury was out only four hours and returned a verdict of guilty as charged on October 24, 1927. Cammarata and Licavoli were remanded to custody and scheduled to be sentenced the following day by Justice William Wright. Wright had been the presiding judge who had sat on the case. The two men could receive up to a maximum sentence of five years in prison on the gun conviction charge.

On October 20, 1927, Wright sentenced Thomas Licavoli and Frank Cammarata to three years each in the Kingston Penitentiary at Portsmouth, Ontario. The two men continued to be held in the Essex County Jail in Sandwich, while their lawyers appealed their convictions to the Appellate Court at Toronto, Ontario. Their appeal was eventually turned down, and their convictions were upheld. On November 28, 1927, Thomas Licavoli and Frank Cammarata entered the Kingston Penitentiary. At the time of their Canadian conviction, both Licavoli and Cammarata were wanted by Detroit police on a charge of assault with intent to kill for an incident involving Nelson Riley, a Detroit policeman who was attacked and beaten on the corner of East Jefferson and Field Avenues on September 7, 1927. His gun and night stick had been taken from him by two men alleged to be Thomas Licavoli and Frank Cammarata.

• • •

Joseph Tallman was a well-know Jewish bootlegger and rumrunner. Tallman had been involved in the Detroit area liquor rackets since the early years of Prohibition and was known in the Detroit underworld as a "Rum Czar." He had partnered with several well-known Detroit area rumrunners and gunmen in the rackets. At one time, Tallman had been in business with Mike Dipisa, a notorious Sicilian gangster who was killed while trying to extort money from a downriver blind pig operator. Tallman and Dipisa had been partners in a Clifford Street blind pig known as the Green Front.

Tallman had also partnered with Joe Moceri in his rum-running business and in several blind pigs. By the mid-'20s, however, Moceri had taken on several new associates as partners, including Pete and Yonnie Licavoli, and Cammarata. Tallman split from Moceri and began operating with an ex-Prohibition agent named Pete Clifford and Sam Rosenberg, a younger brother of Purple Gangster Abe "Buffalo Harry" Rosenberg. Clifford and Tallman were partners in a Third Avenue blind pig.

The exact reason for the split between Joe Tallman and Joe Moceri is not known. The two men and their business associates continued to work together at various times until the spring of 1927. As late as March 9, 1927, Tallman was arrested in the company of a number of men who were associated with the Licavoli/Moceri River Gang. This group included Charles Moceri, Joe Bommarito, Dominic Badalamenti, and Tony Parisi. The men were arrested at the foot of Walker Street in Detroit for violation of the state liquor law. They were stopped by Detroit police and Customs officers, as they were driving away from the riverfront in several trucks that were found to be loaded with liquor, cordials, and bootlegging supplies. The contraband had just landed from Canada. All of the men were eventually convicted on the charge and given a choice of six months in the Detroit House of Corrections or a $500 fine each. They opted for the fine. The Detroit police confiscated a valuable load that included: 688 quarts of whiskey; 240 quarts of whiskey; 36 pints of wine; 168 quarts of champagne; 176 pints of champagne; 118 pints of brandy; 36 quarts of gin; 180 gallons of whiskey malt; 200 quarts of whiskey; 480 gallons of whiskey; 24 pints of whiskey; 362 quarts of cordials.

But by early fall of 1927, there were indications that Tallman and Moceri were at odds. The feud was first evidenced when a boat that was owned by Moceri's River Gang was rammed and sunk by one of Joe Tallman's boats. The incident occurred in the Detroit River near Peche Island. According to Detroit police officials, Tallman had been operating independently of the River Gang for several months. His boats had been hijacked a number of times during this period. He had supposedly rammed the

Moceri boat to prevent another hijacking of one of his loads.

The hijacking of Tallman's boats by the River Gang and the boat-ramming incident were only the beginning of the trouble. On October 11, 1927, four truckloads of Tallman's liquor en route from Port Huron, Michigan, to Detroit were hijacked by members of the River Gang. The trucks were stopped just outside the Detroit city limits on Harper Road. The hijacking had been well planned. Traffic was stopped on Harper Road at the point of sawed-off shotguns and pistols, while all four trucks were commandeered by the River Gang. All of the drivers were taken to Detroit and later released. All of them except for Tallman's new business associate Sam Rosenberg, that is. The River Gang made off with 100 cases of Tallman's liquor valued at $25,000. Rosenberg was kidnapped and taken to a room in a rundown hotel at Randolph and Atwater Streets in Detroit. He was held captive by the River Gang with a ransom of $10,000 demanded for his release. Tallman's other drivers were reportedly beaten by the River Gang and warned to keep their mouths shut before they were released.

Members of the Detroit Police Department's Black Hand Squad told reporters that they had received information that the hijacking of Tallman's trucks and the kidnapping of Rosenberg had been engineered by Thomas Licavoli and Frank Cammarata from their jail cell in Ontario, Canada. The purpose of the hijacking and kidnapping was to raise the $15,000 bail each that was required by Canadian authorities to release the two men on bond. This theory was probably accurate as Tallman had broken with his old partners and had already engaged in several skirmishes with the River Gang.

Moceri and Licavoli had underestimated Tallman. Joe Tallman was a physically tough man who stood over six feet in height and prided himself in settling his problems with his fists. He was never known to carry a gun. Tallman found out where Rosenberg was being held and, accompanied by one of his lieutenants, Oscar Wuester, went to the rooming house and physically overpowered the three men who were guarding Rosenberg. Rosenberg was released, and Tallman took the three guards as hostages.

Sam Rosenberg's older brother Abe had notified the Detroit police when Sam had failed to return home the night of October 11, 1927. Interestingly, this was not Sam's first kidnapping. Both Abe and Sam Rosenberg had been kidnapped in early September 1927. The Rosenberg brothers had been abducted at gunpoint as they were walking down Hastings Street. Abe, who had been armed at the time of the kidnapping, never had a chance to use his gun. The two men were rumored to have been held captive for five days and released only after they had paid a $25,000 ransom. At the time, local newspapers speculated that the kidnappers were "New York gunmen." It is more likely that the Rosenbergs had actually been kidnapped by the "Legs" Laman kidnapping Mob of Detroit. The Laman gang was engaged in the very profitable business of kidnapping local wiseguys and holding them for ransom.

After Sam Rosenberg was rescued by Tallman and Wuester, he was picked up by the Detroit police for questioning. Acting on information received from Sam Rosenberg, police raided the rooming house where Rosenberg had claimed to have been held and arrested nine men. Sam Rosenberg identified three of the nine men arrested as the men who had been involved in the hijacking and kidnapping plots. They were James Licavoli, Joe Moceri, and William Steinberg. Sam Rosenberg was scheduled to appear at police headquarters on October 12, 1927, to sign a deposition. He failed to appear and his brother Abe came in his place to tell police that Sam was out of town. The case against Licavoli, Steinberg, and Moceri was dropped when Sam Rosenberg failed to appear as a witness against the three men, and they were released. A *Detroit Times* article mistakenly printed that Sam Rosenberg had been rescued by the police. The story of how Joe Tallman had freed Rosenberg did not come out until several years later.

In the meantime, Tallman had taken his hostages to an apartment on Third Avenue in Detroit where they were held prisoner. Tallman held the three men captive for 10 days according to underworld rumors. One of the hostages was reported to be Pete Licavoli himself. Finally, Tallman's old partner Mike Dipisa went to Tallman and offered to be the intermediary between Tallman and the River Gang to aid in negotiating for the release of the three gangsters. An agreement was reached, and Tallman's 100 cases of hijacked liquor were returned to him and the hostages were released.

The agreement was supposed to be a peace gesture between the River Gang and Tallman, but by that time, Tallman may have already been a marked man. The River Gang leaders had always suspected Joe Tallman as the person who had made the anonymous phone call to the Windsor, Ontario, police headquarters. This was the tip that led to the arrest and eventual conviction of Thomas Licavoli and Frank Cammarata on the Canadian gun charge.

On November 8, 1927, John "Jack" Burke, one of Tallman's men, was shot to death in a boat well at the foot of Field Avenue in Detroit. Burke had been working on the engine of one of Tallman's speedboats. Two unidentified men walked down a path from Jefferson Avenue and opened fire on Burke and Oscar Wuester. The gunmen had evidently mistaken Burke for Tallman, as the two men bore a striking resemblance. Wuester was also wounded in the attack. Joe Tallman, who was working in another boat well less than 50 feet away, was missed completely.

After "Jack" Burke was shot to death, Tallman was rumored to have paid off Moceri for the boat that Tallman had rammed and sunk off Peche Island. Tallman raised and renovated the boat afterwards. Fearing for his life as a result of repeated incidents, Tallman left for Florida, where he tried his hand in some Gulf Coast rum-running. According to underworld sources, he lost more than $20,000 in his Gulf Coast venture.

In the spring of 1928, Tallman moved back to Detroit and again went into business running beer and liquor from Canada. On April 10, 1928, Pete Clifford, Tallman's partner in a Third Avenue blind pig, was badly wounded and his car riddled with bullets by River Gang gunmen.

On the morning of October 13, 1928, Joseph Tallman was shot to death as he was driving in Detroit. The car in which Tallman and two companions were riding was suddenly forced to the curb by another vehicle in which three gunmen opened fire on Tallman. Tallman's two associates, Harvey Smith and Max Wuester, told police that they had just left a saloon at Third and Selden and were driving south on Fourth Street when the incident occurred. More than 13 shots had been fired. Wuester and Smith, who had been riding in the back seat of Tallman's car, barely escaped injury. Tallman was killed instantly in the attack.

A Detroit Police Department motorcycle patrolman who was in the area heard the shots and attempted to pursue the gunmen's car. He ended up losing track of the car in traffic and pulled over another vehicle that turned out to be the wrong one.

Joe Moceri was suspected by Detroit police of being behind the murder of Tallman. On July 14, 1928, the day after Tallman was murdered, Moceri appeared at police headquarters with his attorney, Miles N. Cullahan. Moceri told the detectives that he and Joe Tallman had been business associates. He admitted that they had worked together for a long time pulling beer. Moceri explained that the sinking of his boat in the upper Detroit River by Joe Tallman was the result of bad feelings that Tallman harbored after Moceri quit him and went into business with other partners. He stated that Tallman had actually been a half owner of the boat that was sunk and had paid Moceri for it. He denied any knowledge of the killing. Moceri would later prove his alibi—he had been on a fishing trip with friends near Strawberry Island on Lake St. Clair the night Tallman was murdered.

• • •

Aside from an ample supply of muscle, part of the success of the River Gang was due to Pete Licavoli's ability to bribe various Customs and law-enforcement officials. The actual landing of liquor on the U.S. shore by boat from Canada was a Customs rather than a Prohibition law violation. Licavoli's success in dealing with U.S. Customs officials continued for several years between 1925 and 1930. Then one night, a U.S. Customs inspector named Charles A. Nixon drank too much in a

Detroit blind pig and began boasting out loud about being on Pete Licavoli's payroll. His remarks were reported to U.S. Customs authorities. Nixon was investigated and later released from the U.S. Customs Service, when it was discovered that he had been taking bribes from rumrunners. This and other similar incidents prompted the U.S. Treasury Department to begin an investigation into the widespread corruption that was rumored to exist in the Detroit area Customs Service. A number of undercover Treasury Department agents were sent to Detroit to infiltrate the ranks of the local U.S. Customs officers and ferret out inspectors taking bribes. In 1928 a special undercover investigator from the Department of the Treasury named Lawrence Fleischman was offered $100 a month by Pete Licavoli. Two other Customs inspectors who worked with Fleischman named Shell Miller and James Mack were offered $200 a month each by Pete Licavoli to "lay off" rumrunners landing cargoes. Fleischman, who later testified against Miller and Mack at their federal trial, claimed that Miller had originally demanded $1,000 a month from Licavoli but later agreed upon the lesser amount.

On November 4, 1929, Peter Licavoli was indicted by a Federal Grand Jury on the charge of bribing a Federal officer. Early in the morning of December 4, 1929, Licavoli was stopped and arrested by Detroit police and U.S. Customs inspectors. Licavoli was in the lead car in a column of four vehicles headed towards Detroit, when he was stopped by the officers on the Belle Isle Bridge. As he was being questioned regarding the federal arrest warrant, he suddenly jerked loose of the officers, jumped into one of the other cars in the column, and escaped in a hail of bullets. At least 20 shots were fired at Licavoli by police and Customs inspectors, with none hitting their mark. Several days after Licavoli had escaped from the officers, the bullet-riddled body of a man known as a local racketeer and rumrunner was fished out of a lagoon near the Scott Fountain at Belle Isle. It was assumed by Detroit police that the unidentified man had been operating on the river without the consent of the River Gang and had paid the price for his insolence.

On the morning of January 2, 1930, an assassination attempt was made on the life of Detroit Police Inspector Henry J. Garvin. The gunmen opened fire with pistols and sawed-off shotguns from another car that sped up alongside Garvin's vehicle and ran it to the curb. Garvin was seriously wounded in the attack. An 11-year-old schoolgirl named Lois Bartlett, who had been near the scene at the time of the shooting, was in critical condition as the result of getting hit by stray shotgun pellets meant for Garvin. The attack on Garvin was followed by an extreme crackdown by the Detroit Police Department on the local underworld.

According to underworld sources, Pete Licavoli decided to voluntarily turn himself in on the U.S. charge rather than possibly be shot on sight by Detroit police who were seeking him as a suspect in the Garvin shooting. The River Gang leaders were all suspects in the attempted murder of Garvin. Pete Licavoli, in the company of his attorney, turned himself in to federal authorities on the bribery warrant. He pleaded not guilty before Federal Judge Edward J. Moinet and was released on a $10,000 bond. He was promptly arrested for investigation by Detroit police officers and taken to police headquarters, where he was questioned about the attack on Garvin. Joe Moceri was also one of many River

Gang mobsters who were arrested and questioned in the police dragnet following the Garvin shooting.

In 1931, Pete Licavoli was named in a second indictment handed down by a federal grand jury for bribing U.S. Customs officers James Mack and Shell Miller and attempting to bribe undercover agent Lawrence Fleischman. Mack and Miller were eventually convicted of accepting money from Licavoli in return for allowing his boats to land their liquor cargoes in the U.S. They were both sentenced to two years in Leavenworth Penitentiary.

Pete Licavoli was also indicted in 1931 by the Buckley Grand Jury in Wayne County for his alleged participation in the murder of Jerry Buckley, a popular WMBC radio commentator. Buckley had been shot to death in the lobby of the LaSalle Hotel in July of 1930. In the fall of 1931, Peter Licavoli was arrested in Toledo, Ohio, and returned to Detroit on October 2, 1931, to face the various charges that were pending against him. He was released for lack of evidence in the Buckley murder case, but in time he stood trial on the U.S. charge. Licavoli was convicted of bribing a U.S. Customs officer as a result of the testimony of undercover Treasury Department Agent Lawrence Fleischman. Fleischman's testimony was corroborated by ex-Customs Inspector Shell Miller, who had already been convicted of taking bribes. On June 22, 1933, Peter Licavoli was sentenced to serve two years in Leavenworth Penitentiary and pay a fine of $1,000.

Joseph Moceri, Roy Pascuzzi, Secretary-Treasurer of the Riverside Brewery Company of Riverside, Ontario, his brother Joe Pascuzzi, and Sam Goldberg, all leaders or business associates of the River Gang, were all convicted of conspiracy to violate the U.S. Prohibition laws in 1930. The four men were sentenced to serve two years each in federal prison. Moceri was fined $3,000, Roy Pascuzzi $5,000, Goldberg $2,000, and Joe Pascuzzi $2,000. The men were sentenced by Judge Edward J. Moinet in Detroit's Federal Court on May 21, 1930. The group had been convicted of operating a liquor syndicate by using boats, trucks, and automobiles for transporting contraband across the Detroit River. The conviction was primarily based on evidence that was obtained when federal Prohibition agents tapped the telephone lines to offices used by various members of the River Gang to run their rum-running and marketing operations. After a number of appeals, the men were finally sent to prison to serve out their sentences. Moceri was convicted on a second liquor law violation while he was still out on bond for the first charge. He was caught in a raid and charged with operating a liquor cutting plant in Grosse Pointe Farms. He pleaded guilty on the second charge and was sentenced by Federal Judge Moinet to serve his second sentence concurrently with the original sentence imposed.

• • •

Frank Cammarata and Thomas "Yonnie" Licavoli were released from Canadian prison in May of 1930 and returned to Detroit. Deportation proceedings were started against Cammarata in early 1931 for entering the United States within five years of having committed a crime.

In February of 1931 Frank Cammarata's legal difficulties were compounded when he was brought to trial for his participation in the People's Bank of Wayne County robbery in 1925. The case was heard before Judge Donald VanZile in Detroit Recorders Court. Cammarata had been the only one of four gunmen originally arrested and formally charged in the robbery case. He was convicted on the original charge and given a 15- to 30-year sentence in the State Prison of Southern Michigan at Jackson on February 26, 1931. His conviction was upheld after several appeals to higher courts. Cammarata's armed-robbery sentence was eventually repealed by Michigan Governor Frank Fitzgerald in 1936, to time served. This was done in order to deport Cammarata to his native Sicily as an undesirable alien.

In January of 1937, Cammarata was deported to Sicily, only to sneak back into the United States in 1939. His presence in the U.S. was not discovered until 1948, when he was picked up with a number of other suspects in a police raid on a Grosse Pointe, Michigan, address.

The fact that Frank Cammarata had been brought to trial on the old armed-robbery charge more than five years after his initial arrest in the case and almost a year after his release from Canadian prison was unique. It had much to do with the Detroit political climate after the assassination of WMBC radio commentator Jerry Buckley in July of 1930. A number of River Gang associates were suspects in the murder, and anyone associated with the Licavoli brothers was put under intense scrutiny by the Buckley Grand Jury. This grand jury had been called to investigate conditions that led to the rampant Detroit crime wave in the summer of 1930.

Thomas Yonnie Licavoli operated in Detroit for a short time after his release from Canadian prison in May of 1930. In early 1931, Yonnie Licavoli and his gang moved their operations to the Toledo, Ohio, area. They immediately began organizing the Toledo and northern Ohio rackets. Yonnie met little resistance from local Toledo racketeers, and those who did not cooperate were quickly eliminated.

A good example of the swift retribution of the Licavoli Mob was the daytime execution of Abe (Abe the Punk) Lubitsky, a numbers operator in the Toledo, Ohio, area. Lubitsky was suspected of giving information to a federal grand jury by Jacob (Firetop) Sulkin, a political fixer for the Licavoli Mob in Toledo. Sulkin believed that Lubitsky had talked because Lubitsky had been given favorable treatment by the federal judge in charge of the grand jury investigation. On October 6, 1931, Lubitsky, Norman (Big Agate) Blatt, and one of their employees named Hyman (Nig) Abrams were driving to Lubitsky's home from a downtown Toledo restaurant. As they stopped for a traffic light, another car pulled up alongside Lubitsky's and several gunmen opened fire with shotguns and pistols. Lubitsky and Blatt were killed. Abrams managed to crawl out of the passenger-side door of the car and roll underneath the vehicle, escaping injury. Lubitsky had been following his brother Morris, who had been in the car in front of his. Morris ran back to find his brother and Blatt mortally wounded. Abe's last words were, "Morris, it was the dagos."

Thomas Yonnie Licavoli and his Ohio Mob rode high for several years until Licavoli and several of his lieutenants were convicted of first-degree murder. The conviction was the final result of the 1933 murder of Jack Kennedy, a popular Toledo blind pig operator and bootlegger. Kennedy had successfully resisted the Licavoli Mob's muscle for a short time. Yonnie was convicted not of pulling the trigger but of being the Mob boss who had set the plan into motion and conspired to kill Kennedy. At that time, this was a novel legal theory on which to base the prosecution's arguments in a murder case. It was one of the first successful prosecutions of a gangland boss based on a conspiracy premise. Licavoli received a life sentence as a result of the conviction. He could have been sentenced to death in the electric chair, but the jury asked for leniency.

• • •

Increased federal Prohibition enforcement on the Detroit River would eventually lead to the demise of the River Gang's profitable liquor hauling business by 1930. This, however, would have little effect on the brewing Mob war that was about to explode in the Detroit underworld in 1930. The dispute would be between the rival Detroit Mafia factions known as the Eastside and Westside Mobs.

# The Fish Market Murders

"Whenever Ches LaMare is going to bump
somebody off he ain't going to tell any copper."
*—Chester LaMare, 1924*

February 17, 1930, was a somber day in
Detroit's Italian community. That morning a
large crowd of people gathered at the Church
of the Most Holy Family in Detroit to pay their last
respects to Salvatore "Sam" Catalanotte.
Catalanotte died several days before in his luxuri-
ous Grosse Pointe home of complications resulting
from pneumonia. His death occurred one day before
his 36th birthday. Sam Catalanotte had developed a
reputation as a kind and charitable man among the
residents of Detroit's "Little Italy." He was rumored
to have amassed a fortune through various business
ventures that was estimated to be almost a million
dollars by the time of his death. Most of this money
had been given away to needy Italians according to
friends of the family. A massive funeral procession of
more than 200 cars left the church following the
mass. The body was laid to rest at Mt. Olivet

51

Cemetery on Detroit's near east side. Several vehicles were required to transport almost $5,000 worth of flowers to the grave site. The funeral was reported to have cost more than $20,000 and was one of the most extravagant in Detroit history. The mourners were a mixed lot that included immediate family, friends of the family, wealthy bankers, merchants, and racketeers.

To the community, Sam Catalanotte was a popular political and business leader who made a comfortable living as Director of the Detroit Italian American Bakery Association. To the underworld, Sam Catalanotte was probably the most powerful and respected Mafia boss in Detroit history. A product of the Giannola/Vitale Gang War of the World War I era, Catalanotte emerged at the end of the conflict as the overseer of the Detroit area Italian underworld. He was a man endowed with great diplomatic ability and charisma. Catalanotte presided over a tenuous peace between the remnants of the Giannola and Vitale Mobs after 1920. As an underworld boss, Catalanotte always preferred peaceful solutions to disputes rather than violence. As a result of his policies, the Detroit area Mafia groups prospered for nearly a decade without bloodshed.

When Sam Catalanotte died in early 1930, there were five organized Mafia gangs in the Detroit area underworld. The two largest organizations were known as the Eastside and the Westside Mobs, and they were both composed of several smaller crime groups. Headed by Angelo Meli, "Black" Leo Cellura, William "Black Bill" Tocco, and Joseph Zerilli, the Eastside group operated east of Detroit and on the upper Detroit River. The notorious Licavoli brothers'

River Gang was also affiliated with the Eastsiders as was a smaller Mob operated out of Wyandotte, led by a downriver mobster named Anthony Danni. The Westside Mob was comprised mostly of members of the old Sam Catalanotte Gang and was led by Chester W. LaMare, the Hamtramck underworld boss. A downriver gang headed by Joseph Tocco (a brother of William "Black Bill" Tocco) was loyal to LaMare and the Westsiders, as was a much smaller downriver outfit headed by Ben (Benny the Baker) Vitagliano. Most of these mobsters were veterans of the Giannola/Vitale Gang War. LaMare, Meli, "Benny the Baker," Sam Catalanotte, Joe Zerilli, and "Black" Leo Cellura had all been associated with the Giannola brothers during the bloodshed.

Sam Catalanotte had two brothers, Joseph and James. Joe Catalanotte was serving a federal prison sentence at the time of Sam's death. James Catalanotte was not well liked or respected among the various underworld groups. At first, it was thought that Angelo Meli would succeed Sam Catalanotte as the "Boss of Bosses," but this situation was prevented from occurring when the treacherous Westside Mob boss, Chester LaMare, made his disastrous bid for power.

Sometimes referred to as the "Vice King" of Hamtramck or the "Capone" of Hamtramck, Chester LaMare was born Caesar LaMare in Chicago, Illinois, in 1884. LaMare's parents were part of the first great wave of immigrants to the U.S. from Sicily and Italy after 1880. He was first arrested in Chicago in 1908 on a larceny charge. In 1911, he was convicted of forgery and sentenced to six months in prison. During his early criminal career in Chicago, LaMare met and befriended a powerful Mafia associate named Anthony Lombardo. Interestingly, Lombardo would later go on to become one of Al Capone's closest advisers. Through the backing of the Capone organization and various intrigues, Lombardo eventually became president of the Unione Siciliane or the Italian-American National Union. Originally founded as a benevolent society to advance the interests of Sicilian immigrants, the organization fell into disrepute by the late '20s when it became dominated by gangsters. The underworld became fond of using the association as a legitimate front for other activities. Lombardo was murdered while president of the organization on September 6, 1928.

Chester LaMare arrived in Detroit in 1915 and became associated with the Giannola Mob. LaMare was an efficient and ruthless gunman. As a result he quickly rose through the ranks of the Giannola gang during the Giannola/Vitale Gang War of 1918-1921. By the time that Sam Giannola was murdered in 1919, LaMare had become his chief lieutenant. Upon Sam Giannola's sudden demise, it was generally believed in the underworld that Chester LaMare would inherit Giannola's prestige and authority.

When the Giannola/Vitale war ended in early 1921, LaMare and two other Giannola gunmen, Angelo Meli and "Black" Leo Cellura, set up shop in Hamtramck, Michigan. Hamtramck was a booming manufacturing center, a city within the city limits of Detroit. The three mobsters formed a partnership and with the Catalanotte Mob as muscle, quickly took control of the liquor and vice rackets in Hamtramck. They opened the glittering Venice Cafe, which became one of Hamtramck's most popular nightclubs. Working under the leadership of Sam Catalanotte, LaMare became the underboss of the Catalanotte gang. This group would eventually become known as the Westside Mob. Under the guidance of LaMare and Meli, the gang prospered, forcing brothels, blind pigs, and gambling operators to pay protection money to their syndicate.

In November of 1922, the Venice Cafe was closed and padlocked by Hamtramck law-enforcement officials. LaMare and Cellura were arrested and charged with violations of the U.S. Prohibition laws. By 1923, conditions in Hamtramck had gotten so rotten and the city government so corrupt that concerned citizens of Hamtramck appealed to Michigan Governor Alex Groesbeck to take action. Exercising his emergency powers, Groesbeck sent a detachment of Michigan State Troopers under Captain Ira Marmon to take over the law enforcement and municipal functions of the Hamtramck city government. The State Police investigation into conditions in Hamtramck uncovered some startling revelations. More than 400 soft-drink parlors licensed by the city sold everything but soft drinks. One hundred and fifty brothels operated around the clock seven days a week. Liquor and beer were sold openly at candy stores, pool rooms, restaurants, and even from cars. Gambling houses ran wide open without police interference. While the Michigan State Police took over the law-enforcement duties, deputies of the Wayne County Sheriff's Department took control of the Hamtramck police station and the City Hall. Gambling operations were quickly shut down. Brothels were raided and blind pigs closed. Nearly 200 raids were conducted in a period of four months. State troopers seized 75 stills, closed two breweries, and destroyed 20,000 gallons of moonshine liquor, 100,000 gallons of mash, 800 half barrels of beer, and more than 7,000 gallons of beer in vats. Governor Groesbeck personally presided over the removal hearing of Hamtramck Mayor Peter C. Jezewski.

Jezewski and 29 others were later indicted by a Federal Grand Jury, convicted of liquor law violations, and sentenced to federal prison. The 30 included Hamtramck Director of Public Safety Max A. Wolinski and Bertha Johnson, a well-known madam and the proprietor of the Hamtramck Inn.

LaMare's underworld operations took substantial financial losses during the state law-enforcement crackdown on Hamtramck. In 1926, LaMare was convicted of the original Prohibition law violation charge that had closed his Venice Cafe in 1922. He had also been indicted in the 1923 Hamtramck beer ring conspiracy case developed by the Michigan State Police after their takeover of Hamtramck. LaMare went on the lam at that time but later surrendered to federal authorities and pleaded not guilty to the charges. He was convicted of violation of the U.S. Prohibition Laws in federal court before Judge Charles E. Simmons on May 25, 1926. LaMare was fined $1,000 and sentenced to one year in federal prison. He was released on a $5,000 bond pending his appeal. In 1927, the U.S. Court of Appeals in Cincinnati upheld LaMare's conviction. Later that year, LaMare was brought before Federal Judge Charles E. Simmons for sentencing. To the amazement of everyone, Judge Simmons added an additional $500 to LaMare's original $1,000 fine and gave him probation. The judge later told the press that he did this on LaMare's promise to "go straight." The ruling was very strange indeed, in light of the fact that by 1927 Chester LaMare had been arrested more than 18 times for such crimes as extortion, armed robbery, Prohibition law violations, carrying concealed weapons, and white slavery. He was sentenced to fines or imprisonment five times. It did not appear that LaMare would be a good probation risk.

In order to maintain his new-found legitimate image, LaMare invested in a fruit concession that sold produce to Ford Motor Company plants in the Detroit area. He was also awarded a car agency franchise that became known as the Crescent Motor Sales. The franchise had been granted to LaMare by Harry Bennett, chief of the infamous Ford Motor Company Service Department. LaMare was able to get these valuable business concessions through the help of Joseph Palma. Palma had once been the head of the U.S. Secret Service Department. He supposedly aided LaMare because the gangster had once informed for the government in some counterfeit cases. By the mid-'20s, LaMare had separated from his original partners, Meli and Cellura, who aligned themselves with the Eastside Mob. Although LaMare's lucrative Ford fruit concession brought him more than $100,000 a year, he still remained active in the rackets.

During his probation, LaMare began to muscle into the downriver handbook business. His tactics were brutal but extremely effective. LaMare would single out a particular handbook operator as his victim. He would then personally visit the man and suggest that he cut LaMare in for 50 percent of his profits. If the bookmaker was reluctant, LaMare would ask the man if he could speak to him outside.

As the two men conversed on the sidewalk, two car-loads of LaMare's gunmen would converge from opposite directions brandishing their guns. LaMare would nod in their direction and say, "How do you like my equipment? Pretty nice, eh?"

If this meeting was not convincing enough, other means would be employed. One stubborn gambling operator was kidnapped, tied up, and driven out to Lake St. Clair one freezing winter day. A hole was chopped through the ice, and a rope was tied around the victim's waist. He was then dropped through the hole into the frigid water. When the gunmen pulled him up, he was more than willing to cooperate with whatever the boss had in mind. He was dropped through the ice a second time just to make sure he was convinced.

LaMare didn't just order his men to be cruel. He personally took charge of the interrogation of a rival gangster with whom he was feuding. The man was unwilling to give LaMare the information that was demanded. Grabbing a rusty handsaw, LaMare went to work on the rival mobster's leg just above the kneecap. The terrified thug quickly told LaMare everything he wanted to know.

By the late '20s, LaMare was making $3,500 a day. Operating extensively in Wyandotte, LaMare set up a chain of small alcohol stills in private homes and paid the homeowners wages to operate them. Once a week, his men would make the rounds and pick up the alcohol.

LaMare seized the opportunity of Catalanotte's death and immediately began to muscle in on the Eastside Mob's lucrative rackets. The tension that resulted from LaMare's aggressive moves brought Detroit's Italian underworld to the brink of open warfare. In an uncharacteristic display of diplomacy, LaMare invited the other leaders of the local Mafia groups to a peace conference. LaMare sent out word through his emissaries that if the bosses of the various factions would agree to attend the meeting, they could settle their differences amiably. This would end the possibility of unnecessary bloodshed. LaMare's idea had merit. None of the Mob bosses wanted a costly war. LaMare, however, had other reasons for luring the Eastside Mob leadership to the peace conference. He planned to hide three gunmen outside of the meeting room. At a given signal, the assassins would rush in and shoot down all of the opposition leaders. LaMare would emerge from the ambush as the supreme boss of the Italian underworld in Detroit.

The peace conference was scheduled to be held in a fish market located at 2739 Vernor Highway in Detroit the afternoon of May 31, 1930. The marketplace was a popular restaurant and rendezvous for the Westside Mob. The grocery and fish market was owned by a man named Philip Gaustello who was an associate of LaMare and the Westside Mob. Gaustello carried on a profitable beer-selling operation out of the market, which he effectively was using as a front for his bootlegging business.

Angelo Meli, the leader of the Eastside Mob, did not trust LaMare. Instead of attending the meeting with other Eastside underworld leaders, he sent two representatives in their place. The two men were Gasper Scibilia, known as the "Peacemaker," and Sam Parina. Both men were respected Mafia counselors. Meli believed that even if LaMare had set a trap for the Eastsiders, these two men would be safe from harm. Scibilia and Parina arrived at the fish market and were seated in a room in the back of the store.

LaMare's two gunmen panicked when they realized that Meli and the Eastside Mob leadership had sent the two underworld counselors to the meeting in their place. Parina and Scibilia were expecting to meet with the Westside Mob leadership. The presence of the two low-ranking Westside gunmen at the market could only mean one thing to the Eastside arbitrators, a trap. Fearing that Parina and Scibilia would detect the set up and report it to Meli and the Eastside Mob, the gunmen did what they thought they had to do.

As the counsellors waited for LaMare and the other leaders of the Catalanotte Mob to arrive, the two gunmen walked into the room and without saying a word, pulled pistols out of their coats and opened fire on the two men. Scibilia was killed instantly. Parina was shot in the chest and abdomen and critically wounded. He was still alive when police arrived at the scene. He was rushed to Detroit Receiving Hospital. Parina told detectives that he and Scibilia had just sat down to eat lunch when two men they had never seen before walked in and started shooting. He stated that he did not know why anyone would want to harm him or Scibilia. Parina died at 3:23 p.m. on May 31, 1930, approximately three hours after the shooting.

Phil Gaustello was seen by witnesses leaving the fish market after the shooting incident. He was quickly arrested and held as a police witness. Another witness named John Kimmel was walking on the opposite side of Vernor when the gunfire erupted. Kimmel told detectives that he heard shots fired and saw two men leave the fish market and walk away down the alley behind the building.

Edmund Ruttenberg, who operated an ice house opposite the fish market, also heard shots and saw two men leaving the building. Both Kimmel and Ruttenberg were taken to police headquarters where they positively identified mug shots of Joe Amico and Joe Locano as the two gunmen they saw leave the fish market after the murders.

Amico and Locano were not apprehended by Detroit police until July 30, 1930, when they were arrested along with other Westside mobsters in a police raid on the Grosse Pointe home of Sam Catalanotte. Joe Amico was a freelance underworld gunman who had once been a member of the Giannola Mob. Amico had then only recently become associated with Chester LaMare and the Westsiders. He was considered to be an unprincipled gunman who sold his services to the highest bidder. Amico was not well trusted by either side until LaMare took him into his confidence and made him his bodyguard. Joe Locano was a gunman and strong-arm man for Joe Tocco's Wyandotte Mob. The Tocco gang was a satellite branch of LaMare's Westside outfit.

Both Amico and Locano were held for trial in the murder of Gaspare Scibilia, after they were arrested on July 30, 1930. This was based on the earlier identification of mug shots by witnesses who were at the scene of the shooting. The Scibilia murder trial opened in Detroit Recorders Court on October 17, 1930. Almost immediately, the state's case against the two men was severely weakened. Both state's witnesses now claimed in open court that they were no longer positive of their original identification of the defendants. They had only seen the backs of the men as they left the rear door of the fish market and walked down an alley. Philip Gaustello, the owner of the market, told the court that Locano and Amico had been in the front of the fish market talking to him when the murders had occurred. Two other men had actually been in the back room talking with Scibilia and Parina. Gaustello named these two men as Ben "Benny the Ape" Sebastiano and Sam Lombino.

The case was given to a jury on October 23, 1930. Both Locano and Amico were acquitted of the murder of Gaspare Scibilia. The jury returned its verdict after deliberating for five hours and 45 minutes. The two men were immediately rearrested for the murder of Sam Parina. Sebastiano was also picked up and held for trial as the third suspect in the Parina case. The second murder trial in the fish market case presented even more confusing evidence to the jury. Now all three defendants, Amico, Locano, and Sebastiano, claimed that they had talked to Scibilia and Parina the day that they were murdered but had stepped out of the room shortly before the two men were shot to death by unknown assassins. The defense attorney, Emil Colombo, was successful at creating enough doubt in the jurors' minds that all three defendants were acquitted after the jury had deliberated for only one hour and a half.

The Fish Market Murders were the spark that exploded into an all-out gang war between the Eastside and Westside Mafia factions. Meli swore to avenge the deaths of his two representatives and vowed that the war would not end until Chester LaMare was dead. There would be no further peace meetings or compromises.

• • •

Gangland executions were often carried out in broad daylight in front of many witnesses. On June 7, 1930, two of LaMare's ace gunmen, Joe and Sam Gaglio, were brutally shot down while changing a tire at a gasoline station at Mack and Mt. Elliot Avenues in Detroit. Another car filled with rival gangsters noticed the two men working on their vehicle and casually pulled up alongside of the men and opened fire. Shortly afterwards, a Meli gunman named Sam Cillufo was shot 11 times in the back when he stopped for a traffic signal on a busy Detroit street. Potential witnesses would quickly forget everything when confronted by police investigators.

Between May 31, 1930 and July 23, 1930, at least 14 men were murdered, all the victims of gangland guns. The high-profile gang war seemed to stop abruptly with the murder of Gerald Buckley on July 23, 1930. Buckley was an extremely popular WMBC radio commentator suspected of having underworld ties. He was shot to death in the lobby of the LaSalle Hotel in Detroit the same night that Detroit citizens voted to recall Mayor Charles Bowles. It was generally believed that Buckley's participation in the recall campaign led to his death. Angelo Livechi, Ted Pizzino, and Joseph (Scarface) Bommarito, all Eastside Mob gunmen, were later tried and acquitted of the Buckley murder. Following Buckley's death was an all-out Detroit police crackdown on the underworld that all but ended the high-profile gangland murders that were occurring with alarming regularity in Detroit. The Buckley Grand Jury was called to investigate both the Buckley murder and the rampant crime conditions in the city. After Buckley was murdered, most of the leadership of both the Eastside and Westside Mobs went into hiding. Their soldiers continued to snipe at each other on the streets, but the gang war took on a much lower profile.

Both the Detroit Police Department and the Eastside Mob were desperately hunting for Chester LaMare. According to underworld rumor, LaMare fled to New York, where he was reported to be under the protection of the powerful New York Mob. Police also learned through informers that LaMare's 17-year-old son Nicholas was kidnapped by the Eastsiders in an effort to draw LaMare out of hiding. This rumor was later proven to be false when Mrs. LaMare told police that her stepson was actually away at school somewhere in the Western U.S.

Despite the findings of the court, Meli found out almost immediately that Joe Amico and Joe Locano were the two Westside gunmen who pulled the triggers in the Scibilia and Parina slayings. Meli sent word to Amico and the other men who were actually involved in the fish market assassinations that unless they put Chester LaMare "on the spot," they would die in his place. Amico was the closest of the plotters to LaMare, and it was Amico who would orchestrate the final betrayal of the boss.

LaMare had turned his house into a veritable fortress since the Crosstown Gang War had begun a year earlier. Attack dogs roamed the grounds and loaded guns were hidden in every room. LaMare needed only to take a step in any direction to put his hands on a loaded pistol or shotgun. He foolishly believed he was safe. On the evening of February 6, 1931, LaMare arrived at his Grandville Avenue home in Detroit with Joseph Girardi, one of his bodyguards. According to a statement later made by

LaMare's wife Anna, the two men sat and conversed in Italian while she made a pot of coffee. After spending some time with his bodyguard, LaMare asked his wife to drive Girardi home. Mrs. LaMare left the house with Girardi at 9:30 p.m. She was gone for almost three hours. Sometime after she left the house, LaMare allowed two men to enter. The two guests were later identified by fingerprints as Joe Amico and Elmer Macklin. Both men were two of LaMare's most trusted aides. As Amico and Macklin sat in the kitchen of the LaMare home talking with the boss, Macklin got up to carry some dirty dishes to the sink. As LaMare turned his head to speak to Amico, Macklin slid a .32 caliber automatic pistol out of his pocket and shot LaMare twice in the head.

Both Amico and Macklin were suspected of the slaying even before their fingerprints were identified on dishes used the night of the murder. Shortly after LaMare's body was found, the Detroit police put out an alert to arrest Amico and Macklin. Detectives got a tip that the two gunmen were leaving town. They rushed to the Michigan Central Station, where they supposedly missed the two thugs by 15 minutes. All points bulletins were circulated, but they proved to be useless as the two gangsters left the southbound train en route.

Mrs. Anna LaMare was one of the first suspects arrested in the murder. Wayne County Assistant Prosecutor Frank G. Schmanske suspected that she might have been involved in the crime. It took Mrs. LaMare more than two and a half hours to drive her husband's bodyguard home. It was during this time that LaMare was conveniently home with no witnesses in the house. The drive of approximately 10 miles round trip should not have taken more than an hour and a half to complete. According to Mrs. LaMare, she left home at 9:30 p.m. and did not return until after midnight. When she walked into the house, she found Chester lying on the kitchen floor with two bullet wounds in the head. At 12:30 a.m., she called the Coolidge police station and summoned officers to the scene. After being held for several days, Anna LaMare was released on a writ by Judge John A. Boyne in Recorders Court on February 9, 1931. She was served with a grand jury summons by Assistant Prosecutor Schmanske before being released from custody.

Both the Detroit Police Department and the grand jury investigators held great hope that a box of personal papers and documents found in LaMare's home might shed some light on his possible connection to corrupt city officials. The box of papers was turned over to the Buckley Grand Jury. Detectives had been hunting LaMare for months to bring him before the jury for questioning. Based on a tip received from an underworld informer, a police raid had been planned on LaMare's home less than six hours after he was murdered. The raid was scheduled for 6 a.m., February 7, 1931.

Chester LaMare was buried after a small funeral service at Mt. Olivet Cemetery. There were almost as many plainclothes detectives at the funeral as there were friends and family. No important underworld leaders were in attendance.

Elmer Macklin was arrested on October 3, 1931, and charged with the slaying of Chester LaMare. On October 14, 1931, Macklin went before Judge John P. Scallen in Detroit Recorders Court for his preliminary examination on the LaMare murder charge. Macklin was held over for trial. His original warrant was later dismissed, and a new warrant charging Macklin, Amico, and Joe Girardi was obtained. In February of 1932, both Joe Amico and Joe Girardi were picked up by Detroit police and held for trial. The three men were arraigned on the murder charge on February 18, 1932.

The LaMare murder trial began before Judge John P. Scallen in Detroit Recorders Court on April 27, 1932. All three defendants were represented by some of the top criminal legal talent available in the city at that time. Joe Amico was represented by Rodney Baxter, Macklin by Van H. Ring, and Girardi by Ralph Baker. The case was declared a mistrial on May 4, 1932. The mistrial motion was based on a question Rodney Baxter asked of Mrs. LaMare, which the prosecution believed was extremely prejudicial to the case. On June 1, 1932, Joe Girardi was dismissed by Judge Scallen from the murder trial due to insufficient evidence. He was endorsed soon afterward as a state's witness but later refused to testify at the trial of Joe Amico and Elmer Macklin. On June 9, 1932, a directed verdict of not guilty was ordered by Henry S. Sweeny in Detroit Recorders Court. The judge stated that he did not believe that there was sufficient evidence available to the prosecution to successfully try the two defendants.

Joe Amico disappeared abruptly in 1937. Detroit police believed he had been taken for a ride as he did not appear at the funeral of his mother. In 1934, Elmer Macklin was convicted of counterfeiting. He later served a six-year prison term on this conviction. Macklin in later years was given a job on Mathew "Mike" Rubino's horse farm in Macomb

County. Rubino was an Eastside Mob gunman during the Crosstown Mob Wars of 1930-31. He later became a boss in the Detroit Mafia family hierarchy.

The Fish Market Murders and resulting Crosstown Mob War ended with the murder of Chester LaMare in 1931. This war was the last major intergang dispute within the Detroit branch of La Cosa Nostra. In the wake of the Crosstown Mob Wars, the modern Detroit Mafia family would be born.

The summer of 1930 marked the beginning of significant changes in the underworld and upper world of Detroit. As the war between Crosstown Mafia gangs for supremacy of the Italian underworld came to a head, the city witnessed the beginning of the Great Depression. The economic effects of the stock market crash were being felt across the nation. As the economy began to collapse, more people found themselves out of work and without the bare necessities of life. High-profile gangland operations tolerated by the public during the boom period of the roaring '20s were no longer acceptable as hopes and dreams were being shattered by the Great Depression. Petty gambling became a way for the working man to pursue his dreams. Numbers operations flourished in the city as did all types of gambling.

The Italian Mafia family that formed as a result of the Crosstown War would prosper in both legal and illegal enterprises for many years beginning during the Great Depression. Pete Licavoli, John Priziola, Angelo Meli, Joseph Zerilli, and William Tocco would form the ruling commission of the Detroit Mafia. As prohibition was repealed, the liquor racket was quickly replaced by the new

Depression-era demand for gambling rackets. And the newly formed Mafia family was there to cash in.

By 1963, the Detroit Mob would be estimated to have infiltrated legal businesses worth more than $50 million a year. This figure was in addition to an estimated minimum income from illegal enterprises of $150 million a year. This included profits from gambling, narcotics, loan sharking, labor racketeering, and extortion.

# The Purple Gang

"These fellows and many others could have been put away years ago if we'd only had witnesses who stood up. That has always been the great problem. To get witnesses who would dare to go into court and testify."

**—James E. McCarty**
**Chief of Detectives**

The Purple Gang began as a juvenile street gang formed during the World War I years in the old Hastings Street section of Detroit's lower east side. The original core group of Purples were the children of predominantly Eastern European Jews who had recently immigrated to the U.S. These young toughs attended the Bishop ungraded school and quickly became a nuisance to area shopkeepers and residents. From petty street crimes such as robbing from hucksters and rolling drunks, the young Purples quickly graduated into the hijacking and extortion rackets. The advent of statewide Prohibition on May 1, 1918 accelerated this process. By the early '20s, the Purples were working for Charles Leiter and Henry Shorr. These two older mobsters essentially became the mentors of the younger Purples, who they used as muscle for their alley brewing racket. Shorr and Leiter operated

71

a legitimate corn sugar outlet known as the Oakland Sugar House, which they used as a front for many illegal operations including hijacking, extortion of local businesses, and setting up large-scale brewing plants in old warehouses and other buildings capable of producing large amounts of beer and whiskey. The Purples also branched out into gambling and the protection rackets. Many Purples had part-time employment in the flourishing Detroit area gambling industry, where they sold their services to wealthy gambling operators to protect their establishments against robbery from other underworld predators.

The Purples really established their reputation in the Detroit underworld as hijackers, and their methods were brutal. Typically, hijacking involved taking a load of liquor and killing everybody with the load. The Purples would then take good-quality Canadian whiskey and cut it. In this manner, one bottle of good whiskey could be made into at least three bottles of cut product. Purple Gang cutting plants were operating all over the city by 1925. These operations went on seven days a week, around the clock, to provide for the growing demands for illegal liquor. In 1925, there were an estimated 25,000 blind pigs operating in Detroit.

By 1925, the Purples were being led by the four Bernstein brothers—Abe, Joe, Ray, and Isadore. Abe Bernstein was always considered to be the leader of the Purple Gang, probably due more to his diplomatic ability in his dealings with city officials and other underworld operators. Joey Bernstein was really the brains behind the Purples during their glory years in the later '20s. It was Joe Bernstein who organized the estimated 700 handbooks (horse-betting parlors) in the city and who controlled the first successful wire service. The wire service provided information to the city handbooks on horse races at tracks across the country and was a necessary service to the handbooks. Subscription to the Bernstein wire service was not an option for handbook operators. They either subscribed or were permanently put out of business.

The Purples were always a very loose confederation of predominantly Jewish gangsters. There were several factions of the Purple Gang. One of the more powerful groups was known as the Little Jewish Navy. This group of Purples was known by this moniker because one of the group, a man named Martin Berg, owned several high-powered speedboats used to haul liquor from Canada. The Little Jewish Navy was led by Sam Solomon, a major Detroit area bookmaker, and "One Armed" Mike Gelfond, a blind pig operator and racketeer. Other members of this group were often used as gunmen by the Bernstein brothers.

After national Prohibition went into effect on January 16, 1920, there was a large influx of gangsters who came to Detroit to cash in on the booming Detroit area liquor trade. This was estimated to be a $250 million a year business in Detroit by 1925. Many of these newly arrived gangsters became associated with the Purples, swelling the numbers of the gang to at least 200 by 1925.

The Purples established a national reputation for ferocity during the so-called Cleaners and Dyers War from 1925 to 1928. A corrupt Federation of Labor president named Francis X. Martel and several Chicago labor racketeers decided to regulate the cleaning and dyeing industry in Detroit by establishing a gangster-controlled wholesalers association. Abe Bernstein and his brother-in-law, Charles Jacoby, were cut in on the deal. Jacoby owned one of the larger cleaning plants in the Detroit area. The Purple Gang was then used to persuade reluctant cleaners and tailors to join the association. Anyone who did not join suffered a visit from the Purples, who would begin by breaking windows, throwing dye on clothing, stench bombing, and general vandalism of a plant. The next step would be fires and dynamite, the beating of pickup drivers, and the theft of truckloads of laundry, which were then sold back to a tailor for a high price. During this three-year period, hundreds of thousands of dollars in property damage was committed against cleaners and tailors who refused to join the association. Several business agents were also murdered. One rumor had it that the Purples got their colorful name during this period because they sometimes threw purple dye on clothing. After a falling out over division of spoils, Martel broke with Jacoby and Bernstein and persuaded several cleaning plant operators to go to the prosecutor. This culminated in the Purple Gang trial of 1928, in which 13 members were tried and acquitted for extortion. The Purple Gang emerged unscathed and created an illusion of invincibility in the minds of the general public.

By 1929, the Purples ruled the Detroit underworld due as much to solid official protection as to their high-profile, strong-arm methods. No underworld operations went on in the Detroit area without kicking back protection money to the Purple Gang. This included gambling, drug peddling, prostitution, rum-running, and alley brewing. As many as 500 murders have been attributed to the Purples.

By 1929, they were selling liquor to both the New York Mob and the Capone organization in Chicago.

The Purple Gang is best known for two massacres. The first, known as the Milaflores Massacre, in March of 1927 involved the machine-gun murder of a freelance Chicago gunman and two of his friends at the Milaflores Apartments in Detroit. The three were lured to the apartment after the Purples discovered that one of the men had killed a primary Purple Gang liquor distributor named Johnny Reid. This was Detroit's first machine-gun slaying, and no one was ever tried for the murders. The second massacre was known as the Collingwood Manor Massacre. In this instance, three members of the Little Jewish Navy faction were lured to an apartment on Collingwood Avenue in Detroit in September 1931 and shot to death by their fellow Purples. This was basically the beginning of the self-destruction of the Purple Gang. The Collingwood Manor Massacre resulted in the first significant convictions against three Purple Gang leaders.

It is interesting to note that all of the 18 Purple Gangsters who met violent deaths between the years 1927 to 1935 were killed by other members of their own gang. This was due as much to greed as it was to lack of organization within the Mob.

The self-destruction process began in 1929 and continued until 1935, when the Purples essentially lost control of the wire service. By 1935, the gang's manpower had all but disappeared due to inter-gang sniping and lengthy prison sentences.

From approximately 1927 to 1932, the Purples operated with impunity in Detroit. Citizens who viewed high-profile street crimes and gave police depositions often perjured themselves on the witness stand, when facing a defendant whom the papers described as a Purple Gangster. Significant convictions to crimes perpetrated by various Purples could not be obtained by local courts until 1930. That year a Purple Gangster was convicted for the first time on a murder charge and sentenced to life in prison. This arrest was a sign of the times. As the effects of the Great Depression set in, the public grew less tolerant of high-profile criminal acts, preferring instead the more low-key vice rackets such as gambling and narcotics. Of course, by this time Detroit's Italian Mafia family had already begun to corner that market. It was the beginning of the end for the Purple Gang.

Although individual Purples continued to operate after 1935, the Purple Gang as an organized entity in the Detroit underworld no longer existed. The rudiments of the modern Detroit La Cosa Nostra organization essentially walked into the void left by the implosion of the Purple Gang.

# 5 The Snatch Racket

"A kidnapper is worse than a murderer and is so recognized in this country today. No more vicious characters exist in this land of ours than those who would kidnap a human being and hold him for ransom."

> —*Judge Edgar S. Vaught,*
> *U.S. Judge for the Western*
> *District of Oklahoma, 1933*

"I know the kidnap racket is bad. But life's a racket anyway. It's dog eat dog."

> —*Joseph "Legs" Laman*

On September 15, 1933, a tall, thin, unassuming-looking man with black hair was picked up by police during a public-enemy sweep in Los Angeles, California. The man gave his name as George Richards and told police that he was employed as a life insurance salesman. Richards was taken to L.A. police headquarters, where he was mugged and fingerprinted. He was officially charged with vagrancy, and his fingerprints were sent out nationally over the teletype. Then came a frantic long-distance telephone call from Detroit, Michigan, police headquarters. Mr. Richards in reality was Joseph "Red" O'Riordan, one of the leaders of the old "Legs" Laman Gang of kidnappers that terrorized Detroit during the waning days of the '20s. The Detroit police had been searching for O'Riordan for more than three years. O'Riordan was the last important member of the "Legs" Laman Gang not dead or in jail. His arrest and extradition to Detroit to stand trial on abduction charges closed the book on the worst gang of kidnappers in Detroit underworld history.

"Red" and his wife Doris had been living quietly in the Los Angeles area for more than three years. O'Riordan's wife told police that they had moved to California for her health. L.A. police had been tipped off about O'Riordan's whereabouts by a 16-year-old L.A. County Jail inmate named Roy Farlow, who just happened to be O'Riordan's stepson.

Although the Purple Gang has often been credited with being the founding fathers of the so-called "snatch racket" (kidnapping for ransom), Detroit during the mid- to late '20s was plagued by a number of other gangs who specialized in this form of terrorism for profit. The "Legs" Laman Gang was one of the most notorious of the Detroit kidnapping Mobs. This group was active for approximately four years, from 1926 to 1930. It was finally crushed by the combined efforts of the Michigan State Police and the Detroit Police Department. A special task force led by Captain Fred G. Armstrong of the Michigan State Police and Lt. Frank Holland of the Detroit Police Department brought about the eventual demise of the gang.

The "Legs" Laman outfit had been known by several different names during its reign of terror: the Burke, Newberry, Reid Mob; the Laman, Andrews, DeLong Gang; and the Hallisey/DeLong Gang. The name changes were a reflection of the names of the various leaders of the group during the different stages of the gang's evolution.

The original kidnapping gang was believed by Detroit Police Department officials to have been organized by Johnny Reid during the mid-'20s. Reid was a transplanted St. Louis gangster and Detroit blind pig operator. He had been associated with the "Egan's Rats" Mob of St. Louis, Missouri, and maintained a close relationship with the gang after moving to Detroit. The original Mob was thought to have included among its members Fred "Killer" Burke, Ezra Milford Jones, Bob Newberry, and Newberry's brother-in-law Joseph "Red" O'Riordan. Burke, Newberry, and Jones were all well-known St. Louis gunmen affiliated with the Egan's Rats Gang. They frequently worked in the Detroit area during the '20s.

It was Johnny Reid who was credited by the Detroit underworld with having originated the idea of kidnapping "wiseguys" (racketeers and gamblers) and holding them for ransom. Reid had reasoned that these underworld characters could be easily abducted, would pay any reasonable amount of money for their release, and would not go to the police.

In December of 1926, Johnny Reid was murdered. This was shortly after he had organized the original Detroit kidnapping Mob. He did not live long enough to reap the rewards of the gang's successful kidnapping spree in the Detroit area during the summer months of 1927. Under the leadership of Burke, Newberry, and O'Riordan, the gang prospered during its first year of operation. They were said to have taken more than $334,200 from their victims during 1927 alone. Among some of the Mob's better known prey were the gambling elite of the Detroit underworld during the Prohibition era. These men included:

| Gambler | Ransom Amount |
| --- | ---: |
| Charles T. "Doc" Brady | 35,000 |
| Meyer (Fish) Bloomfield | 40,000 |
| Lefty Clark (William Bischoff) | 40,000 |
| Johnny Ryan, George (St. Louis Dutch) Weinbrenner, and Danny Sullivan | 50,000 |
| Mort Wertheimer | 30,000 |
| Ruby Mathias | 25,000 |
| Dick Driscoll | 20,000 |
| Joe Klein | 10,000 |
| Louis Rosenbaum | 15,000 |
| Abraham Fein | 14,000 |
| Two Detroit liquor dealers | 30,000 |
| Five Ecorse liquor dealers | 25,000 |

Eventually, Burke, Newberry, and Jones moved on to other rackets, occasionally assisting the Laman Gang in Detroit area kidnappings.

Joseph "Red" O'Riordan was considered by State Police and Detroit police officials to be the "brains" behind what was later known as The "Legs" Laman Gang. O'Riordan was born in St. Louis, Missouri, on February 9, 1890, the son of a recently immigrated Irish couple. He picked up the nickname "Red" as a youngster because of his shock of red hair and ruddy complexion. O'Riordan, according to his own admission, attended parochial schools and a pharmacy college in St. Louis. He came to Detroit in 1916, where he married. He enlisted in the U.S. Army during the First World War, despite poor vision that might have kept him exempt from the draft. After the war, O'Riordan worked as a pharmacist at various drugstores around Detroit.

According to underworld accounts, O'Riordan struck it rich when he invented a formula for taking the cloudiness out of bathtub gin. When bootleggers first began making gin during prohibition, they used tap water and alcohol, which produced a cloudy product. It was easy for customers to spot the phony gin from the real thing. O'Riordan concocted a formula of distilled water and juniper berries that took the cloudiness out of the bootleg gin, producing a clear product that could be more easily passed off as the genuine article. In later years, O'Riordan also operated several blind pigs in Detroit.

O'Riordan's connections to the Egan's Rats Mob and the underworld went back to his childhood in St. Louis. He had grown up with Egan's Rat gunman August (Gus) Winkler. As children, they passed the time engaging in childhood mischief, including throwing stones through the windows of East St. Louis Chinese laundries and other forms of vandalism. Despite O'Riordan's misspent youth, he seemed to follow more conventional patterns of social mobility by staying in school and later attending college, while his childhood friends grew to be safecrackers, thugs, and gunmen.

By 1929, O'Riordan had a Detroit police record of 14 arrests with no convictions. The charges included armed robbery and violations of the state prohibition laws. It is strange that O'Riordan was never arrested as a suspected kidnapper during this period when he was most active in the "Snatch Racket." O'Riordan evidently gained valuable experience in the Burke, Newberry, Reid Mob. After Burke and Newberry left the gang, O'Riordan continued kidnapping Detroit area bootleggers, gamblers, and handbook operators with Stanley DeLong, Henry "Ray" Andrews, and an aggressive local thug named Joseph "Legs" Laman.

Although the kidnapping gang became well known as the "Legs" Laman Gang, its personnel was constantly changing throughout its period of organized activity. Leadership roles in the gang were assumed at various times by Harry Hallisey, Benny Rubenstein, Stanley DeLong, and Jimmy Walters— gangsters, blind pig operators, and gunmen all. The gang was also composed of a number of lesser-known Detroit underworld characters who were at least as vicious as the leaders.

The kidnapping racket was appealing to the Detroit underworld because it was much safer than rum-running, bootlegging, narcotics peddling, and armed robbery. Danger of arrest was minimal because the kidnapping victim almost always refused to talk.

The gang's namesake, Joseph "Legs" Laman, was a career criminal. He was supposedly called Legs because of the length of his limbs, which appeared out of proportion to the rest of his body. Laman was born in Detroit in 1900. His mother and father separated when he was seven years old. There were four children in the Laman family at this time, and his mother, who had been left near destitute, sent Joseph and a sister to live in the St. Francis Orphan Asylum. He spent five years, from age 7 to age 12, at the orphanage. By the age of 12, Laman had become a disciplinary problem. He was sent to the Ford Republic Youth Home where he stayed until he was 15 years old. At 15, he was released and returned home to find that his mother had since remarried. His new stepfather had no use for the boy, and from age 15 Laman was out on his own. As a teenager, Laman worked as a Teamster and for a short time as a structural steel worker. At the advent of Prohibition, he drifted into crime.

By his own account, Laman became a bootlegger and rumrunner around 1920. He was also suspected of hijacking blind pigs. "Legs" Laman went by the aliases of Joseph Laman and Joseph Kable. His Detroit police record included charges for armed robbery, disorderly conduct, and violating the state prohibition laws. Although the Legs Laman Gang would grow to number more than 20 associates, its members often worked in groups of five or six and frequently pulled kidnapping jobs independently of the larger organization.

The underworld in general created its own terminology related to the kidnapping racket. The kidnap victim was referred to as the "package." The "fingerman" was the person who would identify a potential victim for the gang. The "pickup men" would abduct the person. The "prison" or "castle" was where the kidnap victim would be taken to and held prisoner until the ransom was paid to the gang. The "keeper" was the person or persons who guarded the victim and sometimes beat or tortured the prisoner. The "voice" was the person who would negotiate with the blindfolded victim and help with the ransom payment arrangements. The kidnap Mob's "castles" were often located in different cities. At one time or another, the Laman Gang used houses and apartments in Ferndale, Detroit, and Dearborn, Michigan. The gang also used a location in Monroe, Michigan, and an apartment in Toledo, Ohio.

Torture was sometimes resorted to in order to get an uncooperative victim to negotiate for a ransom. One of the Laman Gang's favorite techniques was applying lit cigarettes to the hands and feet of the victim. Sometimes burning matches were used. Eyelashes were pulled out one at a time or knives thrust into the flesh. Another form of diversion often used by the gang was to tie the package—as the victim was referred to—against a wall and shoot at him with pistols. The object of this exercise was to see how close they could come to the victim without actually wounding him. Obviously, it took very little of this type of persuasion to get the victim to do anything that the kidnappers wanted. The kidnapping Mobs developed their own names for these tortures. Burning a victim with cigarettes or cigars was called "toasting"; shooting at a victim, "fancy shooting"; pulling out eyelashes, "plucking"; or threatening a victim with a red-hot poker, "playing poker."

The kidnap gangs would typically be well organized and follow similar modes of operation. Ransoms paid were most often between $5,000 and $25,000, the amount depending on the financial status of the victim or on how sharp a bargain he could drive. The most important member of the kidnap Mob was the fingerman, the name being derived from the fact that he pointed out the Mob's potential victim or put the "finger" on him. The fingerman named the potential victim, found out his financial status, what racket he was in, and his whereabouts at any particular time of the day or night.

Sometimes the Mob would try to extort money from a potential victim by threat of abduction. If the threats failed to produce the desired results, the man would be kidnapped.

The kidnappers' methods were simple. The pick-up men would either abduct the man from his place of business or pick him up at gunpoint near his home. If the victim were in his car, the gangsters would pull up alongside of him and cut him off, forcing his vehicle to a stop. Then men wearing masks or handkerchiefs to cover their faces would pull guns and force their way into the victim's car. The prey would be forced to drive a short distance. At a prearranged spot, the kidnappers would abandon the prisoner's car and get into their own vehicle, often forcing the victim to lie down on the floor of the car. The masks would remain on the gangsters only long enough to blindfold the kidnap victim. Once the kidnappers returned to their own car, another "tail car" would pull in behind and follow them. The purpose of the tail car was to protect the kidnappers in case of trouble, for example blocking the path of a pursuing police car or providing back up fire support in the event of a gun battle. The victim was taken to one of the gang's castles or hideouts, where typically he would be locked up. For two days, no one spoke to the victim or answered any of his questions. Food was placed near the spot where he was chained. On the third day, a carefully masked member of the gang would approach the victim and ask him to write down a list of his friends who might serve as intermediaries in the ransom negotiations. If the man was a racketeer, as were most of the kidnap victims during the early days of the gang's kidnapping activities, the Mob would make contact with the racketeer's business associates or family through a name on the victim's list. Often the person chosen was another racketeer or even someone associated with the kidnappers whose connection was unknown to the victim.

The person that was used as the go-between in the ransom negotiations was called the "Right O Guy." He was often in a racket himself, but a different racket than the kidnap victim. Once the Right O Guy was chosen, the victim was forced to write a ransom note to his business associates or family. The letter would typically state that his life was in peril and that he would be killed or tortured if the ransom money was not forthcoming. After the ransom letter was delivered, one of the gang would contact the victim's family and tell them how much the ransom would be. The original ransom request would always be for some ridiculous amount of money, which the gang knew that the kidnapped man's family could never meet. This often ranged anywhere from $25,000 to $100,000. The high amount demanded for the ransom gave the kidnappers a lot of bargaining power in the negotiations. They would usually end up settling for between $5,000 and $10,000. The kidnap Mob usually knew how much money the victim was worth and often asked for what they considered to be a fair portion of it. The ransom was paid to the Right O Guy who would conduct the actual ransom negotiations with the victim's family. The family or the man's business associates would never see the actual kidnappers in most cases. The money would be paid to the apparent friend of the family who would take it to his confederates. The Right O Guy would be paid off, the gang would get their money, and the kidnapped wise guy would be released.

This system worked fine for the first couple of years, and these types of kidnappings were almost never reported to the police. Surprisingly, when a racketeer or gambler was kidnapped and paid off the gang once, he was usually never bothered again.

When Laman turned against his Mob and became a state's witness in 1930, he described to a Wayne County Grand Jury the structure of his original kidnapping gang. According to Laman, in late 1926 he, Luke Hartman, Henry "Ray" Andrews, Stanley DeLong and his wife, Dude Manual, and a thug named Joe Mariano established a base of operations for their particular group. The original house was located in Dearborn, Michigan. Later, when things began to get hot for the gang, DeLong's home in Ferndale, Michigan, was often used, along with a place in Detroit. Henry Andrews, his wife, and Mrs. DeLong were put in charge of operating the houses and preparing the meals for the victims. Hartman was used as the fingerman, identifying potential victims for the Mob. Laman was one of the pickup men. Mariano was used as the keeper and torturer and Dude Manual as a sort of handyman.

As long as the kidnapping gangs only "snatched" other underworld types, there seemed to be little interference from the police. The kidnapping of underworld characters was so successful that it wasn't long before the Laman Gang got greedy and started abducting wealthy legitimate businessmen.

The gangsters who Detroit Police Department officials believed were responsible for changing the direction of the Laman Gang's kidnapping activities from the "snatching" of local racketeers to wealthy businessmen were Harry Hallisey and Louis Ross. Hallisey operated a popular Detroit blind pig known as the Camel Club. Louis Ross was a Detroit hand-book operator. Both men had many respectable, wealthy patrons among their clientele. As a blind pig operator, Hallisey befriended many wealthy legitimate people. When their inhibitions were loosened by Hallisey's bootleg liquor and beer, they would often confide in Hallisey about their financial situations and personal problems. Ross, as a hand-book operator taking bets, was also in a unique position to determine potential kidnap victims who were financially secure. Both men were in ideal situations to become fingermen for the Laman Gang. While Hallisey avoided being directly involved in the actual kidnappings, he was alleged to have fingered some of the jobs pulled by the Laman Gang.

Stanley DeLong, who posed as a Ferndale, Michigan, barber, was also one of the men who operated behind the scenes in the Laman Gang, making telephone calls and other arrangements for the paying of ransoms. DeLong had a Detroit Police Department record of 15 arrests, which included charges for armed robbery, violation of state prohibition laws, and carrying a concealed weapon. DeLong would later be identified by Joseph "Legs" Laman as the voice of the gang. DeLong had solid connections in the Detroit underworld and later admitted in court testimony that he was close friends and business associates with Purple Gangster George Cordell alias Cordelli. He had also been involved in the bootlegging business with Benny Rubenstein, another member of the Laman Gang. Rubenstein would be later accused of being a combination fingerman and muscleman for the gang.

Another Detroit gangster who played an important role in the fingering and kidnapping of local businessmen for the Laman Gang was a man named Jimmy Walters. Walters, a well-known Irish mobster, operated a Detroit blind pig named the Clover Club. His cabaret was reported to be one of the hangouts of the Laman Gang. Walters was both a colorful and vicious Detroit underworld character. Born in Detroit in 1897, Walters grew up in the predominately Irish community on Detroit's lower southwest side known as "Corktown." His Detroit Police Department record did not begin until January 21, 1921, when he was arrested for disturbing the peace. He would be arrested 12 times between 1921 and 1930 with no convictions. Charges included possession of burglar tools, violations of the U.S. drug laws, and armed robbery. Walters had served with distinction in the U.S. Army during World War I, as a sergeant in the 116th Field Artillery of the U.S. Expeditionary Force. He was known in the Detroit underworld as a fearless and aggressive thug and reputed to be as good with a pistol as he was with his fists. Walters was also known in the underworld as a powerful independent operator, and he was greatly feared by his competitors.

In 1930, he was identified by Detroit police as being one of the largest drug dealers in the Detroit underworld during the later '20s. His other business dealings, including his cabaret and other interests, were supposedly small compared to his drug operation. He had first been linked to the Detroit narcotics trade when he was indicted as a member of the Bill Morton Gang, which controlled the city's narcotics traffic during the early '20s. Walters was known to be a close friend of Joseph "Legs" Laman.

Among his many racket interests, Walters was reported to have had control of the barrel beer trade in certain sections of the city. His involvement with the Legs Laman Gang was strictly one of his sideline activities.

Supposedly, Walters liked his combat experience during the war but disliked authority. He came back to Detroit with a general contempt for the law. These feelings may have been further aggravated when his younger brother, Edward Walters, was shot and killed by a Detroit detective. Walters's brother and another man were caught breaking into a Duffield Street saloon one night in June of 1926.

For some reason, Walters was known to have a particular hatred of the Italian Mob. His fearlessness was demonstrated many times in various underworld encounters. According to one account, one night two tough local strong-arm men known for "shaking down" independent blind pig operators sauntered into Walters's club. They pulled automatic pistols out of their coats and laid them on the table where they were sitting. They then called Walters over to their table and told him, "We're in for a cut of your club." Walters pulled a gun out of his pocket and laid it on the table with the other two pistols. "So you're in and I'm out? All right, let's see you take the place, just go ahead!" The two men reportedly got up and quickly walked out. At one point, Walters's name was so feared that allowing another blind pig operator to use it in reference was enough to scare off most would-be hijackers and shakedown artists.

Walters was never indicted for being a member of the Legs Laman Gang. He was not positively linked with the gang until several months after his murder in 1930. Walters was arrested as a suspect in the Cass kidnapping in July of 1929, but later released due to lack of evidence. He was eventually connected to the Laman Gang, when "Legs" Laman became a state's witness.

On April 13, 1930, Jimmy Walters was shot to death while working on his car in the driveway of his home. His killers were never identified. One underworld rumor that had circulated at the time was that Jimmy had been muscling in on the east side drug trade and was murdered as a result. Walters was mixed up in so many different rackets including beer, drugs, kidnapping, and murder, it was hard to pinpoint with any accuracy which of his many enemies finally eliminated him.

The Michigan State Police and Detroit Police Department created a special task force in June of 1929 to deal with the Detroit kidnapping problem. According to Captain Fred G. Armstrong of the Michigan State Police, the task force was formed for two main reasons. The first reason was due to the terror that the kidnapping gangs generated among the public, and the second because of the general disrespect for law and order that resulted. Often it appeared that an underworld character could do more to get a kidnapping victim released than the police.

For a short time, the Laman Gang had great success kidnapping Detroit area businessmen. Most of their victims were thankful to be released unharmed and were terrified into silence by the threats and warnings of the kidnappers. This period of success ended abruptly with the kidnapping of David Cass, a 23-year-old gambler and the son of a wealthy Detroit real-estate operator. The Cass kidnapping would spell the beginning of the end for the Laman Gang.

At 4 a.m. on the morning of July 22, 1929, the telephone rang at the home of Gerson C. Cass in Detroit. Cass was well known around Detroit as a wealthy land speculator. His son David left the house early Sunday morning July 21, 1929, and had not been heard from since. Cass was worried that evening, as it was unusual for his son to be gone so long without calling home. He hurried to the phone in anticipation of hearing David's voice.

Instead of talking to his son, Cass was shocked to hear a strange voice tell him that David had been kidnapped. He was instructed to look in his mailbox for a note. Cass rushed to the mailbox, where he found a note written in his son's hand. The note was signed by David and demanded a ransom of $25,000 for his release. Gerson Cass, still reeling from the shock of the horrible discovery, picked the telephone back up and acknowledged to the kidnappers that he had read the ransom note. He was warned that his son would be murdered if he notified the police. Cass was then told that he would be contacted later and given further instructions, and the party hung up. Aside from working in his father's business, David Cass was also a part-owner in a handbook place located on Sibley Street just off Woodward Avenue in Detroit. Young Cass was also known as a man who enjoyed nightclubs and gambling. Possibly his peripheral connection with the Detroit underworld led to his kidnapping. Out of fear for his son's life, Gerson Cass followed the kidnappers' instructions implicitly. He never notified the Detroit police about his son's kidnapping.

Gerson Cass continued to get telephone calls

from the kidnappers during the next several days, demanding various amounts for David's release. The gang finally agreed upon the amount of $4,000, payable in 20-dollar bills. On Thursday, July 25, 1929, Gerson Cass was contacted by the kidnappers and instructed to get the ransom money ready. According to Gerson Cass, in a statement later made to Detroit police at approximately 7:45 p.m. that night, he was called and given specific instructions as to where to deliver the ransom money. Cass was told to go to the corner of Linwood Avenue and Chicago Boulevard at exactly 8 p.m. He was instructed to walk west on Chicago towards Linwood and a man would overtake him. When the stranger whispered "number 8," Cass was to hand him the package of ransom money. The Detroit police were tipped off about the kidnapping of David Cass and the time and place of the ransom exchange, shortly before these events were about to unfold. Crime and Bomb Squad Detectives Albert Shapiro, Lloyd Duane, Charles Wood, and George Nosworthy were dispatched to the scene to arrest the man that the gang had sent to pick up the ransom money. The detectives arrived and took up positions near the corner of Linwood Avenue and Chicago Boulevard. Shapiro, Wood, and Duane hid in an alley between Chicago Boulevard and Rochester Avenue. Nosworthy lay down on the lawn of the Sacred Heart Seminary. Nosworthy would later state in his official report about the incident that when the four detectives arrived at the scene, they noticed a man loitering on the corner of Linwood and Chicago Boulevard. The man appeared to be nervous. This suspicious-looking character would later prove to be Legs Laman. The Cass car pulled up to the curb on Chicago

Boulevard about a half block east of Linwood. Gerson Cass got out carrying the package and began walking slowly west toward Linwood. Laman quickly walked up alongside of Gerson Cass and whispered something. Cass handed the ransom money to him. Nosworthy drew his gun and started after Laman. When Legs noticed he was being followed, he took off running towards the alley where Detectives Duane, Wood, and Shapiro were hiding. The officers yelled for Laman to halt. When he kept running, they opened fire. Laman collapsed on the lawn of the Sacred Heart Seminary. Eight shots were fired between Nosworthy and Shapiro, and it was Shapiro who would be credited with bringing Laman down.

Laman had been shot in the back near his spine and was severely wounded and not expected to live. He was taken to Detroit Receiving Hospital and was partially paralyzed as a result of his wounds but later recovered. The Detroit police initially thought that Laman may have been involved in the kidnapping of David Cass entirely on his own. When first questioned by detectives, Laman told the police that he had been hired by a bootlegger named Jack Kelson to pick up the money from Gerson Cass as part of a liquor transaction. Laman told the police several different stories. At one point, he stated that he was in desperate need of money and had planned the kidnapping himself. When it later became apparent to detectives that Laman was not involved in the Cass kidnapping alone, he refused to name his accomplices. At one point, however, he did tell the police that Cass was not in any danger and that he would not be harmed by the gang, as they would not have anything to gain at that time by hurting Cass,

Laman adding, "They're too yellow to hurt him."

On Saturday, July 27, 1929, a combined force of Detroit Police Department detectives and Dearborn police officers busted into a house in Dearborn, Michigan. The building turned out to be one of the locations used by the Laman Gang to hide their victims. Henry "Ray" Andrews, 31 years old, and his wife Jean, 25 years old, were arrested at the location. The kidnappers' castle had been located by police through the help of a retired Wyandotte bootlegger named Fred Begeman. Several months earlier, Begeman had been one of the victims of the Laman Gang. In an article that had been published in the *Detroit Free Press* two months before, the Laman Gang's Dearborn hideout had been described in detail by an anonymous source who was supposed to be a close associate of some of the gang's victims. In the article, the kidnap victims stated that they had all been chained to a bed in the house. The bed was located in a second-floor room. By stretching the length of their chains, they all reported that they could see a church steeple with a cross on top and the green roof of a nearby building through a crack at the top of the boarded-up bedroom window. When Begeman accompanied police on a tour of the Laman Gang's Dearborn headquarters the day of the raid, he lay on the bed where he had been chained. Through the space at the top of the boarded-up window in the room he could see the church steeple and the green roof that had been described in the earlier *Free Press* article. Begeman also pointed out to the police some writing he had scribbled on the wall of the room in which he had been held prisoner. Begeman identified Laman in Detroit Receiving Hospital as one of the men he had seen enter the room in which he was held at the Dearborn address. Although the room in which Begeman was chained had been kept dark, Begeman identified Henry Andrews as the man who had brought him food. Andrews was identified by his voice. Several sets of handcuffs, leg irons, chains, and a box of dynamite caps were also found by police in the Dearborn house.

The church steeple that had been described by some of the Laman Gang's kidnapping victims was identified later as the top of the St. Alphonsus Catholic Church in Dearborn. A water tank that had also been identified by some of the gang's prisoners was located by police along nearby railroad tracks that could easily be seen from the second-floor bedroom window of the Anthony Street address.

Fred Begeman lived in Wyandotte, Michigan. On April 20, 1929, he was washing his car in the driveway of his home when he was suddenly assaulted by several men who threw a burlap bag over his head. He was trussed up, thrown into a nearby car, and taken to the Anthony Street address. At first, the kidnappers had demanded a $25,000 ransom from Begeman's wife. He was held prisoner for six days in the Dearborn house and finally released for a payment of $5,000. After Begeman was released, the gang continued to harass him. Begeman claimed that he paid the Mob an additional $1,900. The second payment did not satisfy the kidnappers either, and on June 11, 1929, a bomb was thrown onto Begeman's porch, blowing away part of the front of his home. The stress caused by the Laman Gang's extortion techniques finally took its toll on Begeman's family. On July 12, 1929, his wife died of a heart attack. Her doctors blamed her death on the

stress that had been created as a result of the kidnappers' harassment campaign. On July 31, 1929,
Henry Andrews and his wife were officially charged
with kidnapping in the Begeman case.

Shortly after David Cass was kidnapped and
"Legs" Laman had been arrested, Cass's girlfriend
voluntarily appeared at Detroit police headquarters.
She told police that she had been the last person to
see David the night he was abducted. She then
described to police how they had spent their last
night together. The unidentified woman had supposedly accompanied Cass to the Eastwood Inn on
Seven Mile Road in Detroit, for dinner and dancing.
Later that evening, according to her story, Cass
drove downtown and parked in front of the Savoy
Hotel. The woman had gotten out of the car to go to
a nearby drugstore. As she was coming out, she saw
a man she did not know climb into Cass's car. She
got back in, but Cass did not introduce her to the
stranger. Cass then drove his girlfriend to her home.
The unidentified man had never spoken during the
trip, and that was the last time she had seen Cass.

Shortly after Laman was shot down by detectives, the officers picked up two men who had been
waiting at Laman's home. The men were Guy
Tremaine and Andrew Reardon. Reardon was
Laman's brother-in-law. The two men denied know-
ing anything about the Cass kidnapping. They
claimed that they were only waiting for Laman
because they had all made plans to attend a boxing
match that evening. Both men had police records. At
first, police officials believed that they were somehow connected with the kidnapping gang. Upon further investigation, no evidence could be found
against the two men, and they were released. Detroit

police officials hoped that the shooting and arrest of Legs Laman would cause the kidnappers to believe that they had nothing to gain by holding Cass any longer and that he would soon be released. As the days and weeks passed, it became obvious that something more sinister had happened.

In a warrant recommended by Wayne County Prosecutor James E. Chenot, Joseph "Legs" Laman was officially charged with extortion in the Cass kidnapping case on August 7, 1929. Fred Begeman, the ex-Wyandotte bootlegger and previous victim of the gang, positively identified Laman at Receiving Hospital as one of the men he had seen enter the room in which he was held prisoner. Begeman refused to sign the kidnapping complaint against Laman at the time, however, telling police that he wanted to wait until after the trial of Henry "Ray" Andrews. Begeman was probably fearful that Andrews might be acquitted, weakening the case against Laman and putting Begeman in danger of being murdered by the gang in revenge.

• • •

On August 2, 1929, another member of the Laman Gang was arrested in a Toledo, Ohio, apartment. The thug's name was Andrew Germano. Acting on a tip from an informer, members of the Detroit Police Department's Crime and Bomb Squad and Toledo officers located the Toledo, Ohio, base of operations of the Laman Gang. The officers broke into the apartment, surprising Germano, who was carrying three pistols at the time of his arrest. Detroit police officials suspected that Germano was somehow connected with the Cass kidnapping. Once Germano was arrested, he denied any connection with the Laman Gang but admitted to participating in several bank robberies. He also told the arresting officers that he "might have shot a cop or two."

Andrew Germano, like Laman, was a career criminal. Born in Italy in 1900, Germano was brought to the U.S. with his family at age seven and grew up in Flint, Michigan. He was first arrested in Flint for carrying a concealed weapon in 1920. In late November of 1921, Germano was convicted of armed robbery as a consequence of participating in a Flint holdup. On December 3, 1921, he was sent to Marquette Prison. He served five years of his original 10- to 25-year sentence and was paroled on December 31, 1926. While serving time in Marquette, Germano became friendly with two Detroit gangsters named Frank Hohfer and Edward Wiles. Hohfer was serving a 10 to 25 year sentence on an armed-robbery conviction. Wiles had been convicted of breaking and entering and sentenced to 10 to 15 years in prison in Flint, Michigan. It is likely that Hohfer may have originally befriended Henry "Ray" Andrews when the two were serving time together in Jackson Prison. Andrews had served some time during the early '20s on an auto theft conviction. He was released but later returned to prison as a parole violator. It was a result of Hohfer's connection with Henry Andrews that Germano, Hohfer, and Wiles would eventually become associated with the Laman Gang.

Wiles was paroled on February 26, 1928, and returned to Detroit. Frank Hohfer was paroled on May 3, 1929 and was expected to return to Chicago, Illinois, where he had originally lived before coming to Detroit around 1920. If Hohfer did return to Chicago, it was not for long. Hohfer, Wiles, and Germano, along with another ex-convict named

William Cardinal alias Gerald "Skin" Murphy, formed a small gang of freelance bank robbers and kidnappers. They were associated with the Legs Laman Gang and involved in several of the gang's kidnappings. These gangsters formed what the Detroit newspapers would later refer to as an "unholy alliance," while serving time in Marquette Prison. Inspector Henry Garvin would later claim that many of the gang's holdups and kidnappings were actually planned by Germano and the others while they were still behind bars. The gangsters wasted little time in proving that the prison time they served had not reformed their ways.

A good example of the cowboy methods of operation of this group occurred on the night of April 8, 1929. Dr. and Mrs. H.A. St. John were surprised by two men with drawn pistols as they pulled into the garage of their Pontiac, Michigan, home. The men, who had been hiding behind the garage, stepped out of the shadows as the doctor and his wife were getting out of the car. They didn't rob the couple but snatched the car keys away from St. John, shoved him aside, and drove off in his car. Sometime later they stole a set of license plates in Detroit and exchanged them with the plates on the stolen car. The two men who had taken the car had probably been Andrew Germano and Edward Wiles. On the night of April 15, 1929, Germano, Wiles, and another unidentified man drove the stolen car up to Flint, Michigan, where they tried to rob a bank. After an unsuccessful holdup attempt and a shootout with Flint police, they escaped and headed west toward Ann Arbor. The three men were spotted driving aimlessly around the University of Michigan campus by Ann Arbor police officers William Marz and Irwin Keebler at about 2:30 a.m. on April 16, 1929. They looked suspicious, and the officers decided to pull them over. Despite telling a somewhat convincing story, Marz believed the two were up to no good and ordered the man behind the wheel to drive to the Ann Arbor police headquarters. Marz jumped on the running board of the suspects' car to direct them while Keebler followed in the patrol car. When they were several blocks from the police station, the driver of the gangsters' vehicle stepped on the gas and quickly turned down a side street. A man in the back seat pushed an automatic pistol into Marz's stomach and fired four times. He then raised the gun and shot the officer in the chest. A quick curve threw Marz from the running board of the car. Keebler attempted to pursue the outlaws in the scout car but lost them. The only thing that saved Marz's life was that he had been wearing a bullet-proof vest for the first time. The gangsters raced towards Detroit by way of Birmingham. They took a curve too fast on a narrow country road and their car careened off the pavement and overturned onto a large rock formation about two miles north of Twelve Mile on Franklin Road. One of the three men was badly injured in the wreck. All of the gangsters suffered cuts and bruises.

The three men got a ride to the Village of Birmingham. There they walked up to Henry Milldebrandt, a Birmingham police officer who had been standing nearby, and asked him if he could get them a taxi. They explained to Milldebrandt that they had been in an accident and were trying to get back to Detroit. Milldebrandt hailed a taxi. To their surprise, as they piled into the back, Milldebrandt climbed into the front seat and ordered the driver to take them to the Birmingham police station to make out an accident report. When the cab came to a stop behind the station house, one of the men in the back seat, later identified as Germano, pulled a pistol and shot Milldebrandt in the arm. Another man slugged the driver, shoved him toward Milldebrandt, and slid behind the wheel. The police officer was quickly disarmed, and with Germano pointing his gun at the heads of the cabbie and the police officer, the cab squealed off. The two men were bodily thrown from the taxi several blocks from the police station. Later that morning, the stolen cab was found partly submerged in Narrin Lake, two miles southwest of the Village of Ortonville, Michigan. The vehicle was discovered at 6:30 the morning of April 16 by a local woman who lived on a nearby farm. She told police that she saw a second car filled with men drive away from the vicinity of the lake, headed towards Ortonville. The three gangsters completed the evening's events by pulling a stickup in Detroit for some spending money.

Shortly after this rampage, William W. Gunn, the recently retired proprietor of a successful Detroit music store, was shot to death by Laman gangsters in the doorway of his Detroit home. The murder occurred between 9 and 10 p.m. on May 6, 1929. Two men walked up to Gunn's home. When his wife came to the door, they asked her if her husband was in. She called Gunn and when he appeared the gangsters both shoved pistols against his side and, according to Gunn's wife, said, "Come on, we're going for a ride." Gunn grabbed the arm of one of the gunmen and managed to wrestle the gun away from him. The other man calmly shot Gunn twice in the abdomen. According to eyewitnesses, the two men then strolled casually away from the house, got into their car, and drove off. Lt. Holland of the Detroit Police Department Kidnapping Task Force would later state that Gunn had been murdered by Andrew Germano, Edward Wiles, and Lawrence McMullen, another member of the Laman Gang.

· · ·

After arresting Germano in Toledo, Ohio, on August of 1929, the Detroit police were not able to get sufficient evidence to tie him to the kidnapping of David Cass. He later was tried and in October of 1929 convicted for the shooting of Birmingham Patrolman Henry Milldebrandt. The charge was assault with intent to kill and on October 8, 1929, he was sentenced to a 35- to 50-year term in Marquette Prison.

Lawrence McMullen was later convicted of armed robbery in another case and sentenced to five years in the Michigan State Reformatory in Ionia. After the shooting and arrest of "Legs" Laman, events were to happen quickly to bring about the final destruction of the Laman Gang.

On September 11, 1929, two men, later identified as Edward Wiles and Frank Hohfer, rented a furnished apartment in Detroit. These rented rooms were to become the temporary prison of the Laman Gang's next kidnap victim. It would prove to be their last.

Mathew Holdreith was the 24-year-old son of a wealthy Detroit restaurant proprietor. Only several weeks earlier, the senior Holdreith had pointed out Hohfer, who was in the restaurant eating. He identified Hohfer to his family as a former employee who had been sent to prison. Hohfer would later admit to having once worked for Mathew Holdreith's father. Mathew Holdreith was a 1927 graduate of the University of Detroit. After driving his younger brother—a senior at Notre Dame University in Indiana—back to college, Mathew was due to return to Detroit the night of September 11, 1929.

Shortly after renting the apartment, Frank Hohfer called Holdreith's father's home pretending to be a friend of his son. He inquired as to what time Mathew was expected home and was told sometime after 10 p.m. Hohfer, Wiles, and William Cardinal aka Skin Murphy drove over to Holdreith's home and patiently waited for Mathew Holdreith to return from his trip. Mathew later told Detroit police that Hohfer and Wiles were waiting in the backyard of his father's home when he pulled into the driveway sometime after 10:30 p.m. that evening. The gangsters pointed pistols at Holdreith and forced him to walk to their car that was parked a short distance from the house. Holdreith was blindfolded and driven to the kidnappers' new apartment. There he was chained by his hands and feet to a bed and left for the night. The men returned the following day, Thursday, September 12, and released Holdreith from the chains. They ordered him to write a ransom note to his father. At first, he refused and was beaten by the three gangsters. Ultimately, the physical punishment proved to be too much, and he agreed to write the note.

Wiles had been communicating with Holdreith's father. At first the gang had demanded $30,000 for Mathew's freedom. After Holdreith's father had received the ransom note, they eventually agreed on a $5,000 ransom. He was warned repeatedly that if he went to the police, Mathew would be murdered.

The kidnappers then gave his father very specific instructions regarding where and how he was to deliver the ransom money. First, he was to pay the ransom in 20-dollar bills and wrap up the money in brown paper. Then he was told to leave his home at exactly 11:30 p.m. on Saturday, September 14, and, driving no faster than 20 mph, head west on Grand Boulevard to Grand River, taking that to Telegraph Road. At Telegraph and Grand River he would rendezvous with the kidnappers. To be certain he was dealing with the kidnappers, they agreed to toss Mathew's wallet and keys through the open window of his car at the rendezvous location. He would then hand over the package of ransom money.

The night of the scheduled ransom exchange, a Detroit Taxi Company driver named Colman English picked up three men at West Grand Boulevard and 12th Street. The men told the cabbie to drive to Ferndale, where he was directed to Livernois and Marshal Avenues. English was then jumped by the three thugs, robbed, bound, gagged, and thrown into the weeds of a vacant lot. The gangsters then raced off in the stolen cab for their meeting with Holdreith's father. Traveling out Grand River at high speed, they quickly overtook the senior Holdreith, who had been driving slowly to the meeting place as ordered. They followed Holdreith to the intersection of Grand River and Telegraph. At this point they pulled alongside of his car and tossed Mathew's wallet and keys through an open window. They were immediately handed the package of ransom money and drove off. In the meantime, English, after rolling around in the weeds of the Ferndale lot for half an hour, was finally able to free himself. He immediately called the Detroit Police Department and notified them that he had been robbed and his cab stolen. The taxi and license plate numbers were given to the Detroit Police Department's central dispatch.

Early Sunday morning, two Detroit police officers sitting in one of the department's few radio patrol cars spotted the stolen Detroit Taxi Company vehicle go by at about 40 mph. Having just received a report over their car radio regarding the taxi, Patrolmen Hubert McGrath and Edward Fitzgerald gave chase. The man driving the cab stepped on the gas and was seen tossing the package of ransom money out of the window. The officers chased the three gangsters at high speed, when the cab suddenly lurched to a stop and the gangsters opened fire. After a gun battle in which at least 50 shots were exchanged, Wiles and Hohfer, who were both shot and wounded, surrendered. A man later identified as Cardinal escaped on foot in the confusion and was thought to have been wounded. Wiles and Hohfer were arrested and taken to Detroit police headquarters, where they were locked up. Officer Fitzgerald picked up the bag of ransom money, which contained $4,270 dollars in paper currency. What happened to the difference between the $4,270 and $5,000 supposedly asked for is not known.

While all these events were transpiring, Mathew Holdreith was still chained to the bed at the Hanover Street apartment. Sensing that something had happened to the kidnappers, Holdreith tried to get someone's attention by making noise, but no one responded. Finally on Monday, after five days without food or water, Holdreith managed to edge over to the bedroom window and slide it open slightly. His cries for help were heard by a man walking by the building, who called the police. Shortly afterwards, five officers broke into the apartment and released Mathew Holdreith. He was taken to Detroit police headquarters, where he immediately identified Hohfer and Wiles as two of his kidnappers. Up until this time, the two gangsters had refused to answer any questions directed at them by detectives. After Mathew Holdreith positively identified them, they made a full confession. Hohfer confessed to complicity in the kidnapping of David Cass and identified Laman as the leader of the kidnapping gang. Hohfer also told police that he had been with Andrew Germano in Toledo shortly before Germano had been arrested. Wiles and Hohfer implicated William Cardinal alias Skin Murphy in their confessions. Cardinal was still at large. It was later learned that Cardinal was seriously wounded in the shootout with Detroit officers and died of his wounds in Chicago.

While they were being held at Detroit police headquarters for the Holdreith kidnapping, both Wiles and Hohfer were identified by an employee of the Sunny Service Oil Company as the bandits that had held up the company's business offices. Twenty-seven hundred dollars had been taken in the robbery. During the late '20s, kidnapping was still considered a state crime with penalties covered by local statutes. The Michigan laws concerning abduction that were then on the books allowed a judge to give a kidnapper up to 99 years in prison and a $5,000 fine.

The two Detroit police officers who had captured Wiles and Hohfer were later given rewards of $50 each by the Superintendent of Detroit Police and publicly thanked by Mayor John C. Lodge. Both Hohfer and Wiles were tried and quickly convicted in the Holdreith kidnapping case, before Judge Christopher E. Stein in Detroit Recorders Court on October 7, 1929. The jury was out only 30 minutes before bringing in a guilty verdict. The two kidnappers were immediately sentenced by Judge Stein to serve from 30 to 50 years in the State Prison of Northern Michigan at Marquette. This would not be the last time that Hohfer and Wiles would be heard of.

On October 3, 1929, Joseph "Legs" Laman was convicted of extortion in the Cass kidnapping case. The jury was out only two hours and 45 minutes. On October 12, 1929, Laman, yawning and grinning at the court, was sentenced by Recorders Court Judge Christopher Stein to serve from one to two years in the State Prison of Southern Michigan at Jackson. When the judge began to lecture Laman, he yawned and stared at the ceiling. Asked if he had anything to say before sentencing, Laman yelled, "Innocent." When asked by Judge Stein if he wanted to tell him anything about the Cass kidnapping, Laman said, "I don't know anything about it."

Frustrated and enraged by Laman's indifference and his arrogant, smirking attitude throughout the trial, Stein exclaimed, "You're lucky that the maximum penalty for the offense of which you have been found guilty is only two years. It is a pity you were not brought in on the charge of kidnapping rather than extortion. I think that under the same facts you might have been found guilty, and it would have been the privilege of this court to sentence you to life."

Probably feeling slighted by the judge's remarks, Wayne County Prosecutor James E. Chenot took exception to Judge Stein's statement, explaining, "There was not a single shred of evidence against

Laman on a kidnapping charge."

As Laman was being led out of the courtroom, the judge added, "I think you still know a lot about the Cass kidnapping!" Laman just glanced back at the judge with a wide grin on his face.

From the time that Laman had first been arrested in connection with the Cass case, Detroit police officials had continued to leak information to the newspapers that Laman had confessed and implicated other members of the gang. These leaks were an attempt by police to discredit Laman. They wanted to make him look like a turncoat in the eyes of the Detroit underworld. It was also hoped that other members of the gang might believe that Laman had confessed and voluntarily turn themselves in. When Henry Andrews was arrested several days after Laman had been shot, Detroit newspapers carried the story that the police had found Andrews and the Dearborn house through information obtained from Laman when he was arrested. In truth it was Fred Begeman who had led police to the Dearborn address where Andrews and his wife had been arrested.

On October 23, 1929, Henry "Ray" Andrews was found guilty in the kidnapping of retired Wyandotte bootlegger Fred Begeman. On October 31, 1929, Andrews was sentenced by Wayne County Circuit Court Judge Arthur Webster to 35 to 50 years in prison. When asked if he had anything to say before sentencing, Andrews replied, "I'd rather let the matter rest in your hands, I have nothing to say except that I am not guilty."

"Do you mean you are not guilty of this crime but are guilty of others?" Judge Webster asked.

"I am guilty of bootlegging but not of anything of

this sort," Andrews replied.

"Was there any reason why Begeman should have come into this court and to have sworn you were his abductor?" Judge Webster asked.

"Begeman said what the Detroit police wanted him to say, they framed me!" Andrews retorted.

• • •

On October 30, 1929, a trapper checking his lines along the Flint River, about four miles north of Lapeer, Michigan, made a gruesome discovery. As he was walking along the river bank, through the sumac bushes in a ravine between the river and a nearby road, he caught sight of what appeared to be a body. The badly decomposed corpse could not be identified at first. The remains were taken to Lapeer where a local doctor performed an autopsy. Two .32 and two .38 caliber bullets were removed from the body. They had been fired at close range near the heart and were determined to be the immediate cause of death. The body was taken to Detroit the following day, where it was positively identified as being the remains of David Cass.

The identification had been by the Cass family dentist through dental records. Cass had been severely beaten before he was murdered. His jaw had been fractured, and the body was covered with cuts and bruises. When Detroit police began their investigation into the Cass kidnapping in July of 1929, they tried to establish whether there was any trouble between Cass and any Detroit underworld characters. They discovered that David Cass was an addicted gambler, and they believed that he may have given out a number of IOUs that he had welshed on.

Apparently the body of Cass had been carried

from a car parked on nearby Columbiaville Road and thrown off a ravine a distance of about 25 feet down into a stand of sumac bushes along the banks of the Flint River. The badly decomposed state of the body indicated that Cass had probably been killed shortly after being abducted. At first, the brutal murder of David Cass was blamed on Legs Laman, and according to rumors that were being circulated, Laman was to be brought back from Jackson Prison to stand trial for murder. On November 1, 1929, Laman was identified by Fred Begeman as the man who had put a cocked revolver to his head and forced him to write a ransom letter. A friend of Fred Begeman's also identified Laman as one of the men he had paid the ransom to for Begeman's release.

Begeman, who had been the principal witness for the state in the trial of Henry "Ray" Andrews, had originally identified Laman as a member of the gang that had kidnapped him several months earlier. He positively identified Laman in the hospital shortly after Legs had been shot by the police in July of 1929. At that time, Begeman had refused to sign a kidnapping complaint against Laman until Andrews was convicted. Detroit police were also quick to point out that at the time of Legs Laman's conviction on the original extortion charge, the body of David Cass and other important evidence had not yet been found. This was the reason given for only charging Laman with extortion in the Cass kidnapping case, a relatively minor felony compared to kidnapping.

Laman was officially paroled from his extortion sentence so that he could be brought back to Detroit to be tried for kidnapping in the Begeman case. Laman's parole was signed by the governor at the request of the Wayne County prosecutor. If complicity could not be proven in the Begeman kidnapping case, Laman would be returned to Jackson Prison to serve out his extortion sentence. On November 8, 1929, Laman was brought back to Wayne County to be examined on the Begeman kidnapping charge. At his arraignment, Laman pleaded not guilty. On November 14, 1929, Joseph "Legs" Laman was ordered held for trial on the kidnapping charge, after being examined by a Wyandotte Justice of the Peace. A $1-million bond was set for Laman at the request of the Wayne County assistant prosecutor.

In the meantime, crime lab specialists at the Detroit Police Department ran a ballistics test on the pistols that had been taken from Frank Hohfer and Edward Wiles when they surrendered to Detroit police. The test results showed that two of the .32 caliber bullets removed from the body of David Cass had been fired from Hohfer's gun. They also showed that at least one of two .38 caliber bullets taken from the body had been fired from Wiles's pistol. Detroit Police Department detectives presented Wiles and Hohfer with the results of the ballistics test in Marquette Prison. When they were questioned by the police, both Hohfer and Wiles denied that the guns were in their possession at the time David Cass was murdered. Both of these men would later be positively identified as the murderers of David Cass.

The Begeman kidnapping trial was held in Wayne County Circuit Court. During the testimony, Laman was positively identified by Fred Begeman as the man who had forced him at gunpoint to write a ransom letter. Begeman also identified Laman as the person who had called him repeatedly after his initial release and threatened him in an attempt to extort more money. During the trial, Mrs. Henry Andrews admitted to the prosecutors that she and her husband were close friends of Laman and his wife. She also admitted that the Lamans had lived with them for a while at the address in Dearborn. Laman's attorney made a motion for a mistrial during Begeman's testimony because the only identification that Begeman could give was that he recognized Laman's voice. He could not positively state that he could recognize Laman by sight, as the latter had been wearing a handkerchief around the lower part of his face. The motion was denied by Judge Murphy. During the trial, Laman fondled a rabbit's foot that had been given to him by his attorney.

On December 14, 1929, Laman was found guilty of kidnapping in the Begeman case. The jury was out only 55 minutes before returning a guilty verdict. Laman laughed out loud as court officers led him out of the crowded courtroom. Somehow his bravado was not quite as convincing as it had been two months earlier when he had been sentenced on his extortion conviction in the Cass case. On December 21, 1929, Laman was sentenced to 30 to 40 years in the State Prison of Southern Michigan at Jackson.

From the time that Laman had been shot by the police while collecting the ransom money from Gerson Cass, he had been pressured to name his accomplices. Throughout the questioning, Laman had remained stoically silent. Despite the pressure from his peers caused by the false stories that were leaked to the media by the police, it looked like Laman intended to be a "standup guy" and do his time without implicating anyone. But as soon as

Laman was back in Jackson Prison on the kidnapping conviction, Captain Armstrong of the Michigan State Police began visiting him regularly. Armstrong continued to attempt to get Laman to confess and to name the other members of the gang. Exactly why Legs Laman decided to become a state's witness and testify against the rest of the gang is not known for certain. His conviction for kidnapping Begeman and lengthy prison sentence may have helped to put Laman in the frame of mind to expose the rest of the gang. According to one account, Armstrong finally convinced him by promising a reduction in his sentence. It would be Captain Armstrong and Lt. Holland of the Detroit Police Department who were credited with destroying the Laman Gang.

The Laman Gang was reputedly so well organized that its members had agreed to take care of the families of incarcerated gang members. With no means of support, the wives and children of convicted criminals often became destitute and were forced to go on relief. The Laman Gang's arrangement helped relieve the stress on imprisoned gangsters and helped prevent the convicted Mob member from the temptation of turning on the gang as a bargain for a reduction in sentence. Supposedly, when Andrews and Laman were sent to prison, their families had been financially neglected by their former pals. The fact that the gang had turned their backs on the families of Laman and Andrews may have been incentive enough for the two men to become state's witnesses.

According to Harry Bennett, notorious chief of the Ford Motor Company Service Department, "When Laman went to prison, apparently 'Red'

O'Riordan had promised Laman to take care of his wife and daughter. Now two state policemen got hold of Mrs. Laman and the daughter. They mussed the two of them all up and then took them to see Laman. 'This is how much Red O'Riordan thinks of you,' the two officers told Laman. Believing that he had been double-crossed by the gang, Laman turned state's evidence and pointed out everyone involved in the kidnapping of Cass." Bennett claimed that Henry Ford had a profound morbid interest in crime and criminals. He also had a deep sympathy for them. As a result, thousands of ex-convicts were hired by the Ford Motor Company over the years in the name of rehabilitation. This put Harry Bennett in a unique position to have some inside knowledge of the workings of the Detroit underworld. In later years, Bennett would help to get Laman paroled with the promise of a job at Ford.

All of these circumstances evidently had an effect on Laman. He would later state that shortly before he decided to confess and become a witness against his gang, Capt. Armstrong and another officer visited him in his cell. They gave him a copy of a signed statement showing him that Henry Andrews had confessed to his role in the kidnappings of the Laman Gang and had implicated all of the other gangsters. At this point, Laman caved in and also confessed.

In June of 1930, Andrews and Laman were brought to Detroit to testify against their Mob. One revelation followed another. Andrews and Laman told police the details of 14 kidnappings and the murder of David Cass. According to one account, Cass was murdered because of the failure of a deal supposedly made by the gang with Detroit police to trade Cass for the release of Andrews and Laman. This aspect of the case appears to have been an embellishment. There was never any attempt made to trade Cass for the release of Andrews and Laman.

Laman named Walters, himself, William Cardinal aka Skin Murphy, Andrews, Wiles, and Hohfer as being members of the group that had kidnapped and murdered Cass. Jimmy Walters, according to Laman, was the fingerman in the Cass kidnapping. Andrews, Cardinal, Wiles, and Hohfer were the actual kidnappers. Cass had not been kidnapped at the Savoy Hotel as police first thought. He had been picked up near his father's home and taken to a house on Moenart Avenue near Six Mile Road in Detroit. There he was guarded by Hohfer and Wiles, while the ransom negotiations were being completed. When Laman was shot by police while picking up the ransom money, the two thugs had panicked. According to Laman, Wiles, Hohfer, and Cardinal drove Cass to a place near Lapeer. Cass was then ordered out of the car at gunpoint and walked into the woods. Wiles ordered Cass to lie down on the ground. Cass refused and Wiles struck him in the mouth with his pistol. This could explain the fractured jaw found on the body. Cass lay down on the ground, and Wiles patted him on the head. Murphy aka Cardinal, Wiles, and Hohfer then each took turns firing a bullet into the prostrate body of David Cass.

Laman named Jimmy Walters as the fingerman in the Holdreith kidnapping, too, but by June of 1930, Walters had already been killed by rival gangsters. It was also rumored at that time that William Cardinal aka Skin Murphy had died of the wounds he had received when he, Wiles, and Hohfer had a shootout with Detroit police. Laman also confessed that the ransom in the Begeman kidnapping had been split between himself, Andrews, DeLong, and the three others.

Testimony given by Joseph "Legs" Laman and Henry "Ray" Andrews revealed that the Laman Gang had more than 20 associates. During its most successful period, it included: Joseph "Legs" Laman, Stanley DeLong, Benny Rubenstein, Henry "Ray" Andrews, Frank Hohfer, Edward Wiles, Andrew Germano, Roy Cornelius, Jimmy "Jumpy" Kane, Jimmy Walters, Lou Ross, Jerry Mullane, William Cardinal aka Gerald "Skin" Murphy, Harry Hallisey, Virgil Hartman aka Luke Hartman, Joseph "Red" O'Riordan, Edward McMullen, Mariano DeMaria aka Joe Mariano, Emmanual Badalementi aka Dude Manual, Martin Feldman, and Jerry Riley.

The first case in which Laman and Andrews were used as witnesses was the trial of Harry Hallisey, Benny Rubenstein, and Stanley DeLong for the August 2, 1928, kidnapping of Reubin J. Cohen. Cohen was taken to Legs Laman's home in Detroit, where he was chained to the chimney in the attic of the house. The gang wanted a $10,000 ransom for the release of Cohen. DeLong made the arrangements to take Cohen to Laman's home. Reubin Cohen had once been a partner of Benny Rubenstein in the wholesale liquor business. It would be Rubenstein who would pick up the ransom from Cohen's wife, a total of $7,100, and deliver it to the gang. In this job, according to Laman, Kane, Mullane, DeLong, Hallisey, and Cardinal all shared in the ransom money.

During the course of the trial, the defendants'

attorney, Edward Kennedy Jr., asked Laman if he had not lied throughout his entire courtroom testimony in the Cass extortion trial. Laman admitted that he had. Kennedy then asked Laman why he suddenly decided to tell the truth. "They came in," Laman shouted, leaning over the very edge of the witness chair, "and they threw a statement at me. I became so disgusted I talked."

"Whose statement was it?" inquired Kennedy.

"Henry Andrews's statement," replied Laman. "He turned rat the same as I am doing!"

"Do you consider yourself a rat?" asked Kennedy.

"Yes sir, I'm a rat," replied Laman without hesitancy.

"What do you mean by the word rat?" Judge John A. Boyne of Recorders Court inquired.

"It's an underworld term," Laman explained. "It means anyone who squawks and I'm squawking."

During the Cohen trial, DeLong realized the hopelessness of his predicament, pleaded guilty in the Cohen case and joined Laman and Andrews as a witness for the state.

DeLong testified that Joseph "Red" O'Riordan was the leader of the group that kidnapped Reubin Cohen. He claimed that O'Riordan was the first person he talked to about the kidnapping, a week before Cohen had been abducted. DeLong told the court that he had been introduced to O'Riordan and Rubenstein by Harry Hallisey and that Jerry Mullane and Jimmy Kane were also present. The names of O'Riordan and Roy Cornelius had been originally stricken from the warrant by Judge John A. Boyne on a motion from Wayne County Prosecutor James Chenot due to lack of evidence.

During the Cohen kidnapping trial, Rubenstein

admitted to having once been partners in the boot-legging business with Cohen; he also claimed that he knew Purple Gangster George Cordell. According to Rubenstein, DeLong and Cordell were regularly shaking him down for money. When asked by the court how he had gotten the long, deep scar that ran along the cheekbone on the right side of his face, Rubenstein claimed that a Purple Gangster had slashed him. He overheard George Cordell telling someone that he planned to rob a friend of Rubenstein's. Rubenstein warned his friend who then tipped off the police. As a result, one of the holdup men was shot and the other arrested. Rubenstein claimed that about a month later, Cordell returned with several other Purple Gangsters and one of them cut his face. Rubenstein's defense in the Cohen trial was that he had been forced by DeLong to act as the Right O Guy in the Cohen kidnapping. Hallisey swore that he had been in Kenosha, Wisconsin, visiting his parents during the time Cohen was kidnapped.

DeLong had positively connected both Hallisey and Rubenstein to the Cohen kidnapping. During trial testimony, he identified Rubenstein as the fingerman and ransom collector and Hallisey as one of the men who guarded Cohen. On August 24, 1930, after deliberating more than 24 hours, the jury found Rubenstein guilty in the Cohen kidnapping case. Harry Hallisey was acquitted. Hallisey had little time to celebrate his good fortune. He was immediately arrested again and held for trial in the September 7, 1929, kidnapping of Charles Mattler, a Detroit produce merchant. Louis Ross, another Laman gangster, was also held in the Mattler case. At his arraignment on the Mattler kidnapping charge before Recorders Court Judge John V. Brennan, Hallisey stood mute, and a plea of not guilty was entered on his behalf. Jerry Mullane, Benny Rubenstein, Stanley DeLong, Jerry Riley, and Roy Cornelius were also named, along with Hallisey and Ross, in the Mattler kidnapping warrant.

When Mattler was kidnapped, he was asked by the gangsters to name somebody who could be used as the Right O Guy in the ransom negotiations. A minor underworld character named Martin Feldman was used to negotiate Mattler's ransom and the time and place of his release. Feldman, a regular associate of the Laman Gang, was later taken for a ride and burned to death, presumably because he knew too much.

On October 16, 1930, Harry Hallisey, Jerry Mullane, Roy Cornelius, and Lou Ross were all found guilty in the Mattler kidnapping. The guilty verdict had been the culmination of a 10-day-long trial before Judge John A. Boyne in Recorders Court. The jury was out three hours and 45 minutes. The defendants were convicted primarily on the testimony of Laman and Andrews. Hallisey was sentenced to 30 to 40 years in prison with 35 years recommended, Cornelius 20 to 30 years, Ross 35 to 50 years, and Jerry Mullane 30 to 40 years.

Early in August 1931, Edward Wiles, a convicted member of the Laman Gang who was suffering from heart and kidney ailments, threatened Marquette Prison doctor Lowell L. Youngquist. Wiles told Youngquist, "If anything happens to me, my buddies will get you and the rest of your staff." Wiles died in the prison hospital of natural causes on August 6, 1931. On the morning of August 27, 1931, three convicts got into line with other prisoners to see the doctor at 8 a.m. sick call at Marquette Prison. There was only one thing that was unique about these three men. They were all carrying loaded pistols. The group included Andrew Germano, Leo Duver, and Charles Rosbury. Germano, a former member of the Laman Gang, was serving a long sentence for his conviction in the shooting of a Birmingham, Michigan, police officer. Duver was serving life for a Detroit grocery store holdup, and Rosbury 20 to 40 years for an armed-robbery conviction. Frank Hohfer, another convicted Laman Gangster, who was also part of the team, was not allowed to go to sick call with Germano, as the two were close friends. Hohfer remained locked in his E Block cell and secretly armed.

Dr. A.W. Hornbogen, a local Marquette physician, was acting as the prison doctor while Dr. Youngquist was away on vacation. Germano entered the examining room complaining about a pain in his stomach. When Hornbogen told him to take off his shirt to be examined, Germano hesitated, as he had a .32 caliber automatic tucked inside his belt. When the doctor ordered him a second time to take off his shirt, he drew the pistol and shot Hornbogen in the chest at point-blank range. The doctor was killed instantly. The bullet hit him directly in the heart. Frank Oligschlager, a convicted murderer serving a life term who had been working as an attendant at the Marquette Prison Hospital for more than 15 years, grabbed Germano and attempted to wrestle the pistol away from him. At this point, Rosbury and Duver, who had been waiting outside the examining room, rushed in. Duver pulled his pistol and shot Oligschlager in the abdomen. Leo Bulzer, another trustee, was also shot in the leg during the free-for-all.

The hospital, at that time, was located in the center tower of the prison on the third floor, not far from the main gate. At first, it was thought that the convicts were going to try and attempt a breakout from the hospital due to its close proximity to the prison's main gate. After fleeing the hospital, the three convicts then raced down the tower stairs. When they reached the ground floor, they spotted Warden Corgan and Deputy Warden William Newcombe standing at the foot of the stairs talking. As they rushed by, they fired at the startled prison officials. Joe Cowling, an assistant deputy warden who was nearby, was hit in the thigh. The three convicts then forced prison guards Fred Hewlett and George Hurley to unlock doors and accompany them into the prison yard. When they got to the yard, Hurley broke and ran. The convicts started to run after the terrified officer, but the guards on the walls opened fire on the three men, and they raced to the prison industrial building. When the prisoners got to the industrial building, they ran to the second floor of the complex, which was used as a dormitory. Here they grabbed another prison guard named Charles Arenz. In the meantime, a statewide alarm had gone out. All of the State Police at the Marquette barracks and the entire City of Marquette police force were mobilized and rushed to the prison. Extra guards were armed and deputized. One group of officers entered the prison yard, while another formed a cordon around the walls of the prison and watched the roads. A rumor circulated that a group of Detroit gangsters was en route in an armored car to rescue the men if they were able to shoot their way out.

The three convicts exchanged shots with more than 100 officers for almost an hour and a half. Even some of the Marquette Prison trustees were armed as several hundred rounds of ammunition were fired at the convicts' barricade. Near the end of the standoff, Charles Arenz, the prison guard who had been seized by Germano, was forced to write a note to the warden. The note was thrown out a window of the industrial building and read: "The men [Germano and others] have officer and inmates in dormitory under gun and also a quantity of explosives. They are ready to shoot the minute the door is opened. They want big gate opened and have automobile come inside and take them out. They want warden to come in and let them out."

The note was thrown out about 9 a.m. Warden Corgan answered with tear gas shells. When the second tear gas bomb exploded, Rosbury stood up, said, "It's all over, boys," put the gun to his head, and fired. Germano crawled over to Rosbury's body, fired a round into it, and then turned the gun on himself. Duver repeated the actions of the other two men. Shortly after these events had occurred, Hohfer, who was still locked in his E Block cell, pulled out his pistol and fired at a passing wall guard. He then shot himself in the head. Marquette Prison Hospital trustee Frank Oligschlager died of his wounds at midnight August 27, 1931, bringing the total dead to five convicts and Dr. Hornbegen.

As soon as peace was restored in the prison, Warden Corgan and other prison officials immediately began an investigation in order to find out how the guns had been smuggled into the prison. The men had been armed with a .38 caliber Ivers Johnson pistol, a .32 caliber Colt, and two old Spanish revolvers. Marquette Prison officials surmised that the convicts had been hiding the guns for some time in preparation for the prison break. The attempted prison break ended the lives of Germano and Hohfer, two of the Laman Gang's most notorious members.

On Friday, October 6, 1933, Joseph "Red" O'Riordan, last of the fugitive leaders of the Legs Laman Gang, began the long train trip back to Detroit from the West Coast. O'Riordan was in the custody of Detroit Police Department officials. He was being brought back to Detroit to stand trial for the August 1927 kidnapping of Abe Fein, a Detroit blind pig operator. O'Riordan had lost his legal battle against extradition after he had been picked up in Los Angeles during a public-enemy roundup. He was soon identified as a notorious gangster who was wanted by the Detroit police. If for any reason O'Riordan was not convicted in the Fein kidnapping, he would immediately be arrested and held for trial in the Mattler or Cohen kidnapping cases.

During the initial roundup of the Laman Gang in June of 1930, O'Riordan's wife Doris had been picked up by Detroit police and questioned. At the time, she told police officials that she did not know the whereabouts of her husband or anything about his business. By this time Red O'Riordan was already in California. O'Riordan's wife was released and quietly left to join Red in Los Angeles, where they would live under assumed names for the next three years.

O'Riordan was escorted back from the coast chained to two other prisoners. Fred Frahm, Chief of Detectives in the Detroit Police Department, two of his men, and Assistant Wayne County Prosecutor

Herbert E. Munro had gone to Los Angeles to take O'Riordan into custody and bring him back to Detroit. Within an hour of his arrival, O'Riordan was identified at Detroit police headquarters by Abe Fein as one of his abductors. Fein picked O'Riordan out of a lineup of eight men. Fein, who was still working as a blind pig operator at that time, was running an establishment known as the Vernor Inn. O'Riordan by this time was being credited by Detroit police with perfecting the mechanics of the kidnapping racket in Detroit during the late '20s. It was the direct result of Legs Laman's confession three years earlier that would link O'Riordan positively with the kidnapping gang.

O'Riordan had even been suspected of complicity in a plot to kidnap the children of Edsel Ford. According to a confession made by Henry Andrews after he became a state's witness, the gang had planned to use a machine gun to kill the armed guards that constantly protected the Ford children and kidnap the youngsters. Andrews had also claimed that while Hohfer and Wiles were in Marquette Prison, they had sent out instructions to the gang to kidnap the daughters of Fred W. Green, then the Governor of Michigan, and James Corgan, the Marquette Prison warden. According to Andrews, Hohfer and Wiles had written the letter with alum and then written over it with pencil. The letter written in pencil would get past the prison censors. The letter written with alum could not be read until it was pressed out with a flat iron.

On January 22, 1934, O'Riordan's trial began in front of Judge Thomas M. Cotter and a jury in Detroit Recorders Court, nearly seven years after Abe Fein had been kidnapped. O'Riordan was represented by William J. Donovan and Frank Mclain. According to Fein, he had been abducted on July 31, 1927, by Fred "Killer" Burke, Milford Jones, and Red O'Riordan.

By the time of the Fein kidnapping trial, Burke was in Marquette Prison serving a life sentence for murder, and Jones had been dead almost two years, shot to death in a Detroit blind pig by some of his many enemies. According to Fein's testimony, he had walked out of a restaurant after eating breakfast that Sunday morning in 1927. He was getting into a friend's auto when two men jumped on the running board. "Move over, Abe, we got you," said Milford Jones, according to Fein. Fein was shoved from behind the wheel, and his friend was thrown out of the car. Fein claimed that he sat between Jones and O'Riordan. He was blindfolded and driven to a garage. At first, he thought the gangsters were going to take him for a ride. Fein's worried look prompted Jones to say, "Don't worry, Abe, we're only holding you for five grand." Fein stated that he was taken to an apartment later that day, where he was guarded by Burke and Jones. Jones wrote a note to Fein's wife, which Fein was ordered to copy in his own hand. Fein testified that the note read, "Give them anything they want." After Fein copied the note, Jones left with the ransom letter. That was the last he saw Jones. O'Riordan and Burke continued to guard Fein, transferring him to another apartment the following day.

Detroit police were tipped off about the Fein kidnapping shortly after Fein had been "snatched." According to Fein, when Burke found out that the police had been notified, he threatened to kill Fein and called him a "rat" and a "dirty stool pigeon."

Fein told the court that he had begged for his life. His tears evidently prevailed, and later that same day, Fein, Burke, and O'Riordan sat down together amiably and enjoyed a bottle of whiskey.

Fein testified that Purple Gangsters Ray Bernstein, Eddie Fletcher, and Abe Axler were also associated with the kidnapping Mob. At the time of the trial, Ray Bernstein was serving a life sentence, and Fletcher and Axler were dead, having been taken for a ride in November of 1933. When O'Riordan had first been brought back to Detroit in October of 1933, Fein had named only O'Riordan, Burke, and Jones as his kidnappers. He admitted to the court that he had been afraid to name Purple Gangsters Abe Axler and Eddie Fletcher while they were alive. He added that he had not cared to tell the truth about Bernstein. Fein's wife testified that Axler and Fletcher had come to Fein's home shortly after Abe had been kidnapped. The two Purple Gangsters had threatened her. According to Mrs. Fein, Fletcher had said that she should "turn over 25 grand to the captors of your husband." Mrs. Fein borrowed $5,000 from her brother-in-law, which was all that she could raise. She then made arrangements to meet Axler and Fletcher to make the initial payment for her husband's release. They met at Benny Golden's blind pig in Detroit. Mrs. Fein paid the ransom money to Fletcher in the presence of Abe Axler. She admitted that she did not reveal this information to the police while Abe Axler and Eddie Fletcher were still alive. "I wasn't going to take a chance on my life," Mrs. Fein told the court. "They told me never to tell who I paid the money to." Fein was held prisoner by the gang for five days. A total of $14,200 was eventually paid for his release.

On January 25, 1934, O'Riordan was convicted in Recorders Court for the kidnapping of Abe Fein. The jury deliberated for three hours. On February 15, 1934, O'Riordan was sentenced by Judge Cotter to serve from 15 to 45 years in Marquette Prison. After pronouncing sentence, Judge Cotter said to O'Riordan, "I want you to serve your sentence like a man."

"Your Honor, I have always been a man," replied O'Riordan.

• • •

In the end, most of the Laman Gang were either killed or sent to prison for long terms:

**Joseph "Legs" Laman**—Convicted of Extortion in the kidnapping of David Cass and sentenced to two years in Jackson Prison. He was returned from prison shortly afterwards and tried and convicted for the kidnapping of Fred Begeman in December of 1929. He was sentenced to 30 to 50 years in prison. He would eventually become a state's witness and testify against the gang.

**Stanley DeLong**—Convicted in the kidnapping of Reubin Cohen and sentenced to 30 to 40 years in prison. Faced with the hopelessness of his situation, DeLong became a state's witness.

**Benny Rubenstein**—Convicted of the kidnapping of Reubin Cohen and sentenced to 25 to 35 years in prison in August 1930.

**Henry "Ray" Andrews**—Convicted in the kidnapping of Fred Begeman and sentenced to 35 to 50 years in prison. Andrews later became a witness for the state.

**Frank Hohfer**—Convicted in the kidnapping of

Matthew Holdreith in October of 1929 and sentenced to 30 to 50 years in prison. Later named as one of the slayers of David Cass but never brought to trial for the Cass murder. Hohfer was also named by Laman as one of the men involved in the murder of William Gunn in 1929. Hohfer killed himself in Marquette Prison after an unsuccessful prison break attempt August 27, 1931.

**Edward Wiles**—Convicted in the kidnapping of Mathew Holdreith and sentenced to 30 to 50 years in prison. Also named by Laman as one of the men involved in both the Gunn and Cass murders. Died of natural causes, Marquette Prison, August 6, 1931.

**Andrew Germano**—Convicted in the 1929 shooting of a Birmingham, Michigan, police officer and sentenced to 30 to 50 years in prison. Also implicated as one of the murderers of William Gunn. Killed himself in Marquette prison after unsuccessful prison-break attempt on August 27, 1931.

**Roy Cornelius**—Found guilty in the Mattler kidnapping and given 20 to 30 years in prison.

**Jimmy "Jumpy" Kane**—Given a life sentence for his role in a Millberg, Michigan, bank robbery.

**Jimmy Walters**—Shot to death by unidentified gangsters in the driveway of his Detroit home on April 13, 1930.

**Louis Ross**—Found guilty in the Charles Mattler kidnapping and sentenced to 35 to 50 years in prison.

**Jerry Mullane**—Found guilty in the kidnapping of Charles Mattler and sentenced to 30 to 40 years in prison.

**William Cardinal** aka Gerald "Skin" Murphy—

Shot in a gun battle by Detroit police. He later died of his wounds.

**Virgil Hartman** aka Luke Hartman—Convicted in the Begeman kidnapping and sentenced to 15 to 30 years in prison.

**Joseph "Red" O'Riordan**—Implicated in the Fein, Mattler, and Cohen kidnappings. Convicted in the kidnapping of Abe Fein and sentenced to 15 to 45 years.

**Martin Feldman**—Connected to the kidnapping of Charles Mattler by Legs Laman. Laman claimed that Feldman was one of the fingermen. Later taken for a ride and burned to death.

As a result of their testimony, Laman, Andrews, and DeLong were subsequently granted reductions in their original sentences by Michigan Governor William Bruckner. Laman's original sentence of 30 to 40 years was reduced to 10 to 20. Andrews's original sentence of 25 to 50 years was reduced to 20 to 40 years, and DeLong's sentence was reduced from 30 to 40 years to 15 to 30 years in prison.

Many years later, in his autobiography, Harry Bennett, ex-chief of the Ford Motor Company's Service Department, explained how he had first met Legs Laman. In 1929, when the Detroit police were desperately looking for leads in the Cass kidnapping case, Bennett was supposedly contacted and asked if he could get any information. Because the Ford Service Department employed many ex-Detroit gangsters at that time, Bennett was thought to have a handle on what was going on in the Detroit underworld. One night while he was driving home from the plant, Bennett noticed a car parked on a curve in the road, where police often waited to ambush bootleggers. Bennett pulled off the road to talk to the officers, when he noticed the lights immediately go out in what he had thought was a police car. Suspecting trouble, Bennett slouched down in the seat of the car. Suddenly, a shotgun blast blew out his windshield. He stopped the car and got out. Bennett noticed there were four men sitting in the dark car. According to Bennett, "One of these men walked up to me and shoved a shotgun in my belly. He said, 'You S.O.B., you're looking for information, aren't you?' The man on the other end of the gun was Joseph 'Legs' Laman. I talked like 16 lawyers for what seemed like eternity, but it could not have been over 10 minutes." Laman eventually took the shotgun off of Bennett and walked back to the car, leaving Bennett shaken but alive. The men then drove off.

After Laman's prison sentence was reduced, both he and DeLong were offered jobs at Ford Motor Company by Bennett, who helped to get them their paroles. According to Bennett, "I got Laman in my office. I told him, 'You know, the only reason I got you out is that you could have killed me that night and you didn't.' Laman looked at me coldly and said, 'Oh no, if I'd had another slug in my gun you'd have got it!' I believe there was something of a silence after this remark," Bennett would later state. The reformed Legs Laman soon faded into obscurity.

Sam Giannola, last of the three Giannolas killed during the Giannola/Vitale Gang War.

(Photo courtesy of the *Detroit News* collections at the Walter Reuther Library, Wayne State University)

Chester "the Racket King of Hamtramck" LaMare and wife.

(Photo courtesy of the *Detroit News* collections at the Walter Reuther Library, Wayne State University)

Detective Sergeant Emmanuel Roggers, was an undercover officer working on the Detroit Police Department's Black Hand Squad.

(Photo courtesy of the author's collection)

Angelo Meli. Meli was a gunman during the Giannola/Vitale Gang War.

(Photo courtesy of the author's collection)

This is one of the earliest known photographs of Detroit Mafia boss Joseph Zerilli. Zerilli was also a product of the Giannola/Vitale War.

(Photo courtesy of the author's collection)

seph Zerilli (his name is misspelled in photo) and William "Black Bill" Tocco during the police investigation of the Chester LaMare murder February 1931.

(Photo courtesy of the author's collection)

William "Black Bill" Tocco during the Kefauver hearings 1950-51.

(Photo courtesy of the *Detroit News* collections at the Walter Reuther Library, Wayne State University)

Frankie Cammarata. Cammarata was a River Gang gunman and bank robber. He was later deported.

(Photo courtesy of the author's collection)

A late twenties Detroit Police show up photo of a number of important Detroit Italian mob figures. Included is Peter Corrado (far left) and Thomas "Yonny" Licavoli (second from left).

(Photo courtesy of the author's collection)

A late twenties Detroit Police show up photo of members of the River Gang. Joe :eri (second from left) and the Licavoli brothers were the leaders of the River Gang.

(Photo courtesy of  the author's collection)

Peter Licavoli shown in a 1935 mug shot.

(Photo courtesy of the author's collection)

Joe Zerilli in his prime. He eventually became the principle boss of the Detroit area Mafia family and one of the most powerful underworld figures in the country.

(Photo courtesy of the *Detroit News* collections at the Walter Reuther Library, Wayne State University)

James Licavoli, a cousin of Pete and Thomas Licavoli, worked as a gunman for the River Gang. He later became boss of the Cleveland, Ohio mob.

(Photo courtesy of the author's collection)

Elmer Macklin pulled the trigger on Chester LaMare in 1931.

(Photo courtesy of the author's collection)

Joseph Massei, second from left, an important leader of the River Gang, pictured here with Purple Gang attorney Edward Kennedy Jr. in derby to Massei's right.

(Photo courtesy of the collections of the *Detroit News* at the Walter Reuther Library, Wayne State University)

Joseph "Scarface" Bommarito, was a key suspect in the July 1930 murder of WMBC radio commentator Gerald Buckley. He later was a Capo and street enforcer for the Italian mob.

(Photo courtesy of the archives of the State of Michigan)

Joseph "Red" O'Riordan. O'Riordan was a leader of the "Legs" Laman kidnapping mob.

(Photo courtesy of the archives of the State of Michigan)

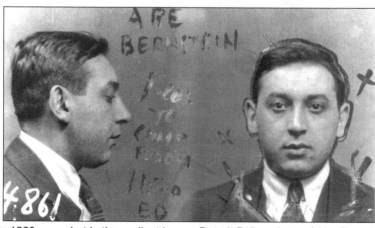

This 1920 mug shot is the earliest known Detroit Police photo of Abe Bernstein, reputed leader of the Purple Gang.

(Photo courtesy of the *Detroit News* collections at the Walter Reuther Library, Wayne State University)

Thomas Camp, better known to history as Fred "Killer" Burke, was one of the founders of what later became the "Legs" Laman kidnapping mob.

(Photo courtesy of the author's collection)

Joseph "Legs" Laman standing center of photo with smirk.

(Photo courtesy of the *Detroit News* collections at the Walter Reuther Library, Wayne State University)

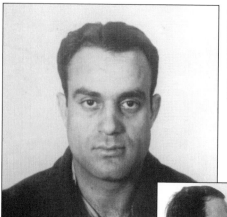

Andrew Germano. Germano was a member of the "Legs" Laman mob known for his viciousness. He committed suicide during a 1931 Marquette Prison riot.

(Photo courtesy of the archives of the State of Michigan)

Frank Hohfer was a Laman mob gunman and one of two Laman mobsters who murdered kidnap victim David Cass.

(Photo courtesy of the archives of the State of Michigan)

Henry "Ray" Andrews. Andrews was a member of the Laman mob. He and his wife kept the houses or kidnap castles where kidnapping victims were taken. He later became a State's witness and testified against the gang.

(Photo courtesy of the archives of the State of Michigan)

Paul Jaworski and his gang were some of the most ruthless bank robbers and payroll robbers of the twentieth century. Jaworski died in the electric chair in 1929.

(Photo courtesy of the *Detroit News* collections at the Walter Reuther Library, Wayne State University)

Stanley "Big Stack" Podolski was a member of the notorious "Shotgun Gang" that robbed banks in the Detroit area during the early twenties.

(Photo courtesy of the archives of the State of Michigan)

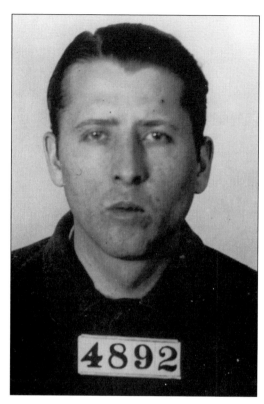

Edward Wiles was a Laman mob gunman. He was the other trigger man in the David Cass murder. He died of natural causes in Marquette Prison shortly before the 1931 riot.

(Photo courtesy of the archives of the State of Michigan)

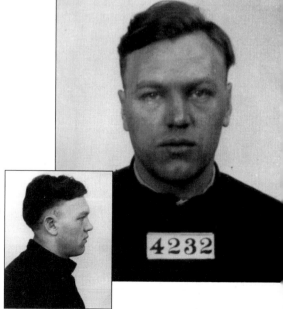

Jimmy Carson was the brains behind the Carson/Kozak mob of bank robbers. Working out of Hamtramck, this gang terrorized southeastern Michigan in the twenties.

(Photo courtesy of the archives of the State of Michigan)

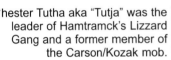

Phillip "Russian Shorty" Kozak was co-leader of the Carson/Kozak mob. His chief value was as a ruthless enforcer for the gang. He was later deported to his native Russia.

(Photo courtesy of the archives of the State of Michigan)

hester Tutha aka "Tutja" was the leader of Hamtramck's Lizzard Gang and a former member of the Carson/Kozak mob.

Photo courtesy of the archives of the state of Michigan)

Special Prosecutor Chester P. O'Hara, left, and Wayne County Circuit Judge Homer Ferguson. Judge Ferguson was appointed a one-man grand juror to investigate charges of corruption in the Detroit Police Department.

(Photo courtesy of the Burton Historical Collection, Detroit Public Library)

Elmer "Buff" Ryan. Ryan was the **I** man who delivered graft protectior payments from the Detroit underw to police and city officials.

(Photo courtesy of the collections the *Detroit News* at the Walter Reuther Library, Wayne State University)

Detroit Police Inspector Raymond Boettcher, January 16, 1940. Boettcher's career was destroyed by the Ferguson Grand Jury investigation. He later became a State's witness.

(Photo courtesy of the collections of the *Detroit News* at the Walter Reuther Library, Wayne State University)

Former Detroit Mayor Rich Reading being fingerprinte Detroit Police headquarters April 24, 1940. Both Readir and his son were convicted and sent to prison as a res of the Ferguson Grand Jur investigation.

(Photo courtesy of the colle tions of the *Detroit News* at Walter Reuther Library, Wa State University)

Dr. Martin Robinson, M.D./bookmaker. A phony robbery at Robinson's office touched off a series of events that started the Ferguson Grand Jury investigation.

(Photo courtesy of the collections of the *Detroit News* at the Walter Reuther Library, Wayne State University)

Everett Watson, September 15, 1941. Watson was a major Detroit numbers operator whose business was destroyed as a result of the Ferguson Grand Jury investigation.

(Photo courtesy of the collections of the *Detroit News* at the Walter Reuther Library, Wayne State University)

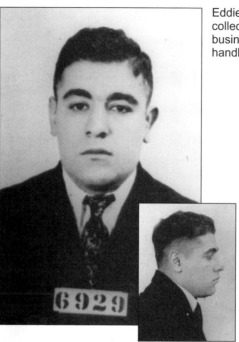

Eddie Sarkesian was a tough Detroit [bill] collector who went into the unhealthy business of robbing Mafia protected handbooks. He paid with his life.

Chris Scroy was a bookmaker and racketeer. His brother Sam and a cousin were murdered by the Detroit mob in 1948 when they tried to set up an independent gambling operation.

# Bank Robbers and Assorted Racketeers

"How many coppers did I get today? Only one you say, that's too bad. I had always hoped to get six of them before they got me. They got me today buddy!"
        —*Paul Jaworski, September 13, 1928*

The morning of June 6, 1928, was typical of an early summer's day in southeastern Michigan. The weather was mild, and a light rain was falling. At approximately 11 a.m., a sedan pulled up in front of the *Detroit News* building located on West Lafayette Boulevard. Five men climbed out of the car, while another man continued to sit behind the wheel. The men were all well dressed. One of them carried a large package wrapped in red paper. The only thing that looked out of the ordinary about the group was that they all seemed to have their hats pulled down over their faces. An attendant inside the lobby of the *Detroit News* building paid little attention to the men, as they walked briskly past his information desk and trotted up the staircase to the second floor of the building. When they reached the second-floor landing, the man carrying the package ripped it open. The package contained three sawed-off shotguns, which were quickly distributed to the others. The sound of shotgun shells being racked into chambers echoed down the stairway corridors of the building. Two of the bandits pulled pistols and walked over to the entrance of the editorial offices. Each of the men quietly took up positions at the doorway, menacing the *News* staff on duty that morning with their guns. The other three men walked into the *Detroit News* business offices located across a hallway. All three gunmen quickly jumped up on a long counter that ran almost the entire length of the large room ending at the cashier's cage. The sound of typewriters and conversations abruptly ceased as one of the bandits yelled, "Put 'em up!" The two other gunmen ran the length of the counter and scaled a 10-foot framed glass partition that separated the cashier's office from the rest of the room. There were about 50 people in the *News* business offices that morning. Most of them were women stenographers. All hands were instantly held high in the air on the gunman's command. The marauders had suddenly turned a routine morning into a terrifying nightmare. One of the ladies in the group edged quietly toward a nearby fire box and tried to pull an alarm. The bandit standing on top of the counter noticed the movement and screamed, "Get away from there!" firing a pistol at the floor and creating a tremendous commotion in the room. One of the two bandits who had dropped down into the cashier's cage held a shotgun on the four employees who were working at that location. Another bandit dumped a box of pay envelopes into a satchel and grabbed at loose bills laying on the countertops, shoving them into his pockets.

While the outlaws were busy in the *News* business offices stuffing pay envelopes into their satchels, Mrs. Mary Lunger, an elevator operator at the *News*, stopped her car on the second floor. The two gangsters who had been guarding the entrances to the editorial offices heard the floor bell ring as the elevator came to a stop. One of them ran over to the elevator entrance and waited for the doors to open. Unaware that there was a robbery in progress, Lunger opened the doors of her elevator car. Instantly, the gunman lunged through the opening and grabbed hold of the terrified woman's arm, attempting to pull her out of the car. Lunger panicked and jerked free of her assailant's grasp, throwing a door stick at the outlaw. She slammed the elevator doors and took it quickly down to the first-floor lobby. As the car doors opened, she screamed to the lobby attendant and another employee of the *News* that the business offices were being robbed. Both men ran out the Lafayette entrance of the building for help. Their cries for help caught the attention of a Detroit police traffic officer who was posted at the corner. He was told by the men to come quickly.

By this time, the bandits had walked out of the cashier's cage and were backing out of the business office. One of the gunmen yelled into the room that an alarm had been given. All five bandits raced down the exit stairway toward the lobby. The attendant in the lobby attempted to close an iron gate that ran across the Lafayette entrance, effectively locking the gangsters into the building. Patrolman George Barstad, who had been on duty directing traffic at the corner of Second and Lafayette, parked his traffic semaphore at the curb. At this point, the five bandits came pounding down the staircase into the lobby. One of them raced up to Sloan, who was still struggling with the gate. Shoving a pistol into Sloan's side, the gunman yelled, "Lookout!" Sloan jumped aside.

Officer Barstad opened the outside door to the vestibule at the same time that the first bandit entered the foyer. The outlaw carried a sawed-off shotgun in his right arm and a satchel in his left. Coming face to face with Barstad, he leveled the shotgun and pulled the trigger. Barstad went down in an explosion of flame and smoke. A *News* employee who was directly behind the police officer was also struck by the pellets and fell. The gunman plunged through the doorway and ran for the sedan that had brought the bandits, now parked on the opposite side of Lafayette. The next bandit through the door stopped long enough to fire two more rounds into the prostrate body of the police officer. According to witnesses, one of the other outlaws was heard making the remark, "Don't let him play possum this time. Make sure he's dead."

As the gunmen were running for the getaway car, Detroit Police Patrolman Guyot W. Craig was walking out of a poolroom located directly across Lafayette Boulevard from the *News* building. In Craig's official report of the incident, he claimed that he had stepped into the poolroom to get his raincoat. As he was walking out, he noticed the five bandits running towards the sedan and Barstad and another man lying wounded on the Lafayette entrance steps to the *News* building. Spotting a youngster nearby, he ordered the boy to lie down behind a telegraph pole. Craig then pulled his revolver from under his rain slicker and opened fire on the bandits. Craig would later state that he first took aim at the gunman who was carrying the shotgun and the satchel. He fired and the outlaw appeared to slip and fall on the sidewalk next to the getaway car. Another bandit jumped out of the car and pulled the wounded man into the sedan.

At this point, several of the other gunmen opened fire on Craig with shotguns and pistols. Craig continued shooting until he emptied his gun, ducking back into a building to reload. Craig was wounded in the left foot during the gun battle. Barstad, the other police officer at the scene, had been shot in the right eye, abdomen, and right arm, and was in critical condition. The *News* employee who had been just behind Barstad when he entered the building was wounded in the hand by the same shotgun charge that had hit Barstad.

The bandits' car roared west on Lafayette, followed by a Detroit Police Department scout car that had just arrived at the scene of the carnage. The scout car was driven by Officer James Moffet, who pursued the bandits for more than 10 miles at high speed. He eventually lost sight of the gunmen's car, which swerved down a side street off Vernor Highway. While Moffet was in pursuit of the bandits' vehicle, the gunmen broke out the rear window of the car and began shooting at the police officer. Moffet thought that at least one of the men in the getaway car appeared to be badly wounded.

A large crowd had witnessed the gunfight in front of the *Detroit News* building. It was estimated that at least 100 people were in the immediate area. Miraculously, none of the observers were wounded. Patrolman George Barstad was rushed to Detroit Receiving Hospital, where doctors held little hope for his recovery.

The car used by the bandits in the *Detroit News* robbery was discovered the following day, when police received a phone call from a garage owner who operated a filling station on the corner of Grand River and Littlefield Avenues in Detroit. He had heard a description of the vehicle and the license numbers over the radio. He told police that around noon on the day of the robbery, he noticed two men wearing raincoats and caps park the car on Littlefield. This was just across the street from his gas station. He stated that he hadn't paid much attention to the car until he heard the description of the vehicle on a radio broadcast about the robbery. Police soon discovered that the car had been stolen from the home of an Albert E. Stewart. Stewart, who was employed as a Supervisor of Properties for the Detroit Public Schools, had reported the car missing on May 20. The original license plates had been switched for a pair taken off a vehicle that was scrapped on May 1, 1928, and sold to the Independent Auto Parts Company in Detroit.

Rewards offered for the capture and conviction of the *Detroit News* bandits totaled $13,000. The *Detroit News* offered $6,000 dollars of the reward money, or $1,000 for the capture and conviction of each of the bandits. The *Detroit Times* offered $1,000 for the capture and conviction of the outlaws. A $6,000 reward was also approved by the Wayne County Board of Auditors.

The Detroit Police Department investigators believed that the bandits were probably Detroiters as they seemed to be very familiar with the layout of the city's streets. According to one account, $25,000 in *Detroit News* payroll money was taken in the holdup. The *News* holdup was characterized as the most daring crime in Detroit history at that time.

The Paul Jaworski Gang was immediately suspected of having been involved in the holdup. An anonymous woman caller had reportedly tipped off the Detroit police that Jaworski had been seen in the city shortly before the holdup occurred. *Detroit News* employees that were eyewitnesses to the robbery were shown mug shots of Paul Jaworski and various members of his gang shortly after the incident. At first, none of the people present that morning were able to identify Jaworski as being a member of the gang. The man who appeared to be the leader of the gunmen during the holdup had a small mustache and wore glasses. When a Detroit Police Department artist drew a mustache and glasses on a police photo of Paul Jaworski, almost instantly three employees of the *Detroit News* identified Jaworski as the man who had directed the heist.

The positive identification of Paul Jaworski in the *Detroit News* robbery added another $5,000 to the reward money. The additional $5,000 was offered by Pennsylvania authorities. Jaworski and another convicted murderer were both awaiting a death sentence when they shot their way out of the Allegheny County Jail in Pittsburgh on August 18, 1927. The two men had been at large ever since.

• • •

Sometimes referred to as a "product of the back alleys of Hamtramck," Michigan, Paul Jaworski was one of the most notorious bank robbers of the Prohibition era. Throughout his criminal career, Jaworski was known by a number of different aliases: Paul Topps, Paul Paluzwski, and Paul Jaworski.

Jaworski was born Paul Poluszynski in Polish Galicia in 1900. The family immigrated to the United States in 1905, first settling in Butler, Pennsylvania. Paul's father, Thomas Poluszynski, was employed as a carpenter, and Paul grew up in what outwardly appeared to be a stable, working-class environment. He was first arrested as a child for stealing apples in Butler, Pennsylvania, a premonition of things to come. The Poluszynski family later moved to Pittsburgh and eventually settled in Hamtramck, Michigan, around 1915.

As a youngster, Jaworski became passionately interested in aeronautics and supposedly mastered the intricacies of the airplane. During the First World War, he tried to enlist in the U.S. Army air service, first in Detroit and later in Cleveland, Ohio. He was turned down both times. It was reported that as children Paul and his brothers Tom and Sam were all juvenile delinquents, constantly suspected by both the Hamtramck and Detroit police of various crimes by the time they became teenagers. According to a personal interview conducted with Paul's father in 1928, Paul had fallen in with what he described as a bad crowd when the boy was around 16. Paul left home at age 19 and according to his father had no contact with the family after that. The only thing that they knew about him was what they read in the newspapers.

Paul began his early criminal career associating with members of the "Shotgun Gang," which operated out of Hamtramck and robbed banks throughout the Detroit metropolitan area. This group of bank robbers, led by Stanley Gawlick, Frank Parmentye, and Vance Hardy, used sawed-off shotguns in their holdups, as the gang's name implied. Known for their ruthlessness and speed in striking a target, Gawlick would often introduce himself as he walked into a bank with shotgun in hand, yelling, "Well here's Stanley, back again!"

This outfit operated successfully for about one

year, robbing banks and then scattering to various rural hideouts. The gang began to crumble when Parmentye and Gawlick were shot down by police during holdups. Hardy was eventually captured, convicted, and given a long prison sentence for armed robbery. Some of the other members of the Shotgun Gang, including Mike Komieczka aka "Mike the Pug," Stanley "Big Stack" Podolski, and his brother John Podolski, would take charge of the remnants of the Shotgun Gang after its original leaders were killed or sent to prison.

Stanley "Big Stack" Podolski was born in Adron, Pennsylvania, in 1900. Both of his parents had immigrated from Poland. The family moved to Hamtramck, Michigan, around 1912. Like Paul Jaworski, Podolski was also a product of "the back alleys of Hamtramck." Known as "Big Stack" because of his size, 6'2" and 210 pounds, Podolski became a close friend of Paul Jaworski and his mentor in crime. Jaworski and his group of thugs began their criminal careers robbing filling stations in Detroit and Hamtramck. Under the tutelage of Stanley "Big Stack" Podolski, the Jaworski Gang quickly graduated to robbing banks

The Jaworski Gang divided their time between Detroit and Pittsburgh. The Mob began making a name for itself robbing coal company payrolls in Pennsylvania. Part of the gang made its headquarters in Detroit and Hamtramck, Michigan, and another group worked out of rural hideouts in western Pennsylvania. In Pennsylvania, the Jaworski Gang was known as the "Flathead Gang."

The first major robbery attributed to the Jaworski Gang was the 1923 holdup of the Detroit Bank branch at West Fort Street and West End, in which $30,000 was taken. The Mob gained its first national notoriety in the December 23, 1923, holdup of a paymaster for the Pittsburgh Terminal Coal Company Branch at Beadling, Pennsylvania. Ross Dennis, the company paymaster, had picked up a $23,000 payroll from a bank in Beadling. He was en route to a company mine when he was ambushed by members of the Jaworski Gang. Dennis, who was riding a motorcycle, was hit by a shotgun blast from bushes along the side of the road. Wounded, he lost control of his motorcycle and fell to the pavement. As Dennis lay on the pavement badly injured, the gangsters walked out of the cover of the bushes and approached him. The paymaster reached for something in his back pocket. Though it was later discovered that Dennis was not carrying a gun, the bandits assumed he was armed and immediately shot him dead. He had made the mistake of reaching for a handkerchief, probably to wipe the blood from his face. The payroll money was taken from a knapsack slung over Dennis's shoulder.

The Jaworski/Flathead Mob then embarked on a long series of depredations in the Detroit and western Pennsylvania regions. Over a period of approximately six years, the gang was involved in at least 14 known major robberies and scores of other crimes including murder. The gangsters showed no mercy in their dealings with their victims. In a 1924 saloon holdup in Pennsylvania, Paul Jaworski was wounded and spent a month in the hospital under police guard. Given bail, he disappeared. On April 14, 1925, the American State Bank branch in Detroit was robbed by the gang. A young bank teller was shot and killed because he had failed to raise his hands quickly enough to suit the gunmen.

On June 13, 1925, members of the Jaworski Gang held up the Central Savings Bank branch in Detroit. The superstitious Jaworski did not participate in this holdup as the robbery had been planned for a Friday the 13th. Twenty-seven thousand dollars was taken by the bandits in this holdup, but all did not go well. During a gun battle in the aftermath of the robbery, a patrolman named Casimer Kaliszewski was shot to death while pursuing the thugs. Arthur Matchus aka "Matches," Stanley Wykowski, and John Podolski, a brother of Stanley "Big Stack" Podolski, were later arrested in connection with the robbery and shooting. All eventually pled guilty to the murder of the police officer and were sentenced to life in Marquette Prison. Stanley "Big Stack" Podolski was arrested with some other suspects but was able to prove an alibi. He was immediately rearrested and held for the 1923 Detroit Bank job. A teller that worked in the bank positively identified "Big Stack" as one of the holdup men. The Jaworski Gang went to great extremes to have the well-liked Podolski acquitted, even offering the teller/witness $1,000 to change his testimony. The attempt was to no avail, and Stanley Podolski was convicted of armed robbery in Detroit Recorders Court and sentenced on June 19, 1925, to 20 to 40 years in Marquette Prison. These convictions represented the first major blow by law-enforcement agencies against the Jaworski Mob and began the gradual disintegration of the gang.

On November 20, 1925, the gangsters held up a Brinks armored car at Dubois and Franklin Streets in Detroit; $18,000 was taken. During the incident, a Brinks Company guard was killed and another seriously wounded. The guards had been en route to deliver a payroll to the Ainsworth Manufacturing Company. Mike Komieczka aka "Mike the Pug" and Walter Makowski were later arrested in connection with the Brinks holdup and murder. Both men were convicted of first-degree murder and sentenced to life in Marquette Prison.

By far the most spectacular job pulled by the Jaworski Gang was the March 11, 1927, dynamiting of an armored car carrying a mine payroll at Coverdale, Pennsylvania. The road was mined with dynamite the night before the holdup. As the armored car passed over, the charge was ignited. The tremendous explosion that resulted flipped the vehicle over on its back and ripped the armored car almost in half. By some miracle, the guards inside the car escaped death. The force of the explosion blew a waist deep hole in the road. The armored car was carrying a payroll for the Pittsburgh Terminal Coal Company, which for some reason was a favorite target of the Jaworski Gang. The guards were ordered out of the demolished armored car, and a $104,000 payroll was taken. One of the guards had been slow when commanded by one of the bandits to lie face down in the snow and was shot and killed as a result. The gang got away from the crime scene with the payroll.

Several days later, Paul Jaworski was captured without a fight on a farm that was often used by the gang as a hideout. The farm was located in nearby Bentleyville, Pennsylvania. The police had reportedly been tipped off by a rival gangster as to Jaworski's whereabouts. It was during his capture at Bentleyville, Pennsylvania, that Paul Poluszynski received the famous alias of Paul Jaworski. An arresting officer had asked Paul his name, and he said "Smith." Another officer noticed a magazine on the floor of the farmhouse and picked it up. The name Jaworski was written in pencil across the top of the cover of the publication. "You're a liar," the officer told him. "Your name's not Smith, it's Jaworski!" "That name will do as well as any other," replied the bandit. The name stuck. From that time on, the name Jaworski would be synonymous with terror, robbery, and murder throughout the Midwest. Shortly after Jaworski was apprehended, the owner of the farm was arrested at Detroit. He admitted to detectives that the Jaworski Gang had used his farm as a hideout in the past after committing holdups in western Pennsylvania. He denied being a member of the gang and agreed to be brought back to the farm where he was to help officers obtain further evidence against the outlaws.

Shortly after Jaworski was captured, he had been shown a fake telegram stating that an accomplice in the Coverdale robbery had been arrested and had confessed to the crime, implicating Jaworski. The man had supposedly been arrested at Detroit. This news brought a confession from Jaworski. He also agreed to show detectives where he had buried $35,000 of the Coverdale robbery loot. The money represented Jaworski's share of the holdup money, and he had buried it on the Weckowski farm. The location of the $35,000 was then discovered on the farm and dug up by officers. Jaworski was charged with murder after he admitted that the gang was responsible for the Beadling, Pennsylvania, mine payroll holdup in 1923 and the Mollenauer, Pennsylvania, mine payroll holdup in 1925. In both robberies, a guard had been killed. Jaworski confessed that he had been the driver of the getaway car in the Coverdale holdup. Jaworski, the man who owned the farm, and four other members of the gang were indicted at Pittsburgh by the Allegheny County Grand Jury for armed robbery in connection with the Coverdale holdup. Paul Jaworski was also indicted for the two payroll robbery murders. Gang members Felix Furtak, John Herbe, Jack Ross, and Stanley Bodziakowski were named in the robbery indictment but not apprehended.

Jaworski pled guilty in both the robberies and the murders. He was first convicted of armed robbery at Pittsburgh and sentenced to 30-60 years in prison on April 11, 1927. He requested that he be brought in front of the grand jury to plead guilty to one of the two homicides to which he had confessed so that he could "have his troubles over with." He was given his wish. Tried for murder in the slaying of a payroll guard during the December 24, 1925, holdup of the Pittsburgh Terminal Coal Company at Mollenauer, Pennsylvania, Jaworski was convicted of first-degree murder on May 18, 1927. He was later sentenced to die in the electric chair.

On August 18, 1927, Paul Jaworski and another convicted murderer named John Vassbinder shot their way out of the Allegheny County Jail at Pittsburgh and escaped. Vassbinder, like Jaworski, was also awaiting the execution of a death sentence. The pistols that Jaworski and Vassbinder used in their "blastout" were believed by police to have been delivered to Jaworski by a visitor to the jail shortly before the escape occurred. Paul Jaworski would later claim that he had bribed an official at the Allegheny County Jail and had gotten two guns as part of the deal. He was allowed to go into an area of the jail called the "bullpen," where prisoners could receive visitors. It was here that a man handed Paul two pistols through the bars. The man, whose identity was unknown at the time, supposedly had been allowed to take the pistols through jail security without being searched. Jaworski claimed he paid $3,000 dollars to the anonymous jail official to allow this to happen. After the man handed the two pistols to Paul, he produced two more revolvers that he would use. Then Jaworski, his mysterious visitor and John Vassbinder shot their way out of the jail. Two guards were badly wounded in the jailbreak. One of the guards would later die as a result of his wounds.

Later, a letter was intercepted by police in Montevideo, Uruguay. It was sent from Detroit by a Sam Tallas to a fugitive bank robber named Jim Mesheek. The letter, which was postmarked shortly before Paul Jaworski had escaped from jail, read in part: "Jim, this may be the last letter I will write to you because I'm going to the jail with four guns. I will give two to Paul and two for myself and we are going to shoot our way out. If we get out we may be down to see you and if we don't it's the graveyard."

As it turns out, the letter was written by Paul's brother, Sam Jaworski. It was signed with the alias Sam Tallas. The return address on the correspondence was 2727 Yemans Avenue, Hamtramck, Michigan. This street number was the home of Paul and Sam Jaworski's parents.

Coincidentally, a search had begun in Detroit for Sam Jaworski, shortly after the jailbreak, in connection with the $5,000 robbery of the General Baking Company on September 9, 1927. He was identified as one of the holdup men by a witness who worked for General Baking Company. At this point, the letter had not yet been discovered, and police still suspected Jaworski's sister of orchestrating the escape.

On August 29, 1927, a man using the name C.S. Stark called on the home of Mrs. Mary Bastuba on 4439 Baldwin Avenue in Detroit. He wanted to rent her garage. Mrs. Bastuba agreed but was suspicious of Stark. One night soon afterward, Mrs. Bastuba's daughter Helen noticed the light on in the garage. Peering through the window, she noticed Stark and another man changing the license plates on a car. Miss Bastuba went to the McClellan police station and notified police of the incident. At the woman's insistence, the precinct sent an officer to watch the garage. On December 30, 1927, the two men returned and were immediately arrested.

C.S. Stark proved to be Sam Jaworski and the other man was Harry Watson. Both men had Detroit police records. They were charged with armed robbery and held for trial. Watson was later identified by Paul Jaworski as one of the six men who had robbed the business offices of the *Detroit News* on June 6, 1928. It was while Sam Jaworski and Harry Watson were sitting in the Wayne County Jail that the incriminating letter was discovered. The letter tied Sam directly to the jailbreak, and he was extradited to Pittsburgh, Pennsylvania. Watson was later released due to lack of evidence.

Sam Jaworski was indicted at Pittsburgh on six different felony counts for helping Paul and Vassbinder escape from the Allegheny County Jail. Sam was later convicted and sentenced to 11-22 years in the Western Pennsylvania Penitentiary.

Paul Jaworski remained at large for more than a

year. In 1928 he participated in at least two holdups. On June 6, 1928, he led the bandits who held up the *Detroit News* business offices. He was also suspected by the Detroit police of being one of the five bandits who held up the business office of the General Baking Company in Detroit on September 9, 1927. Jaworski managed to effectively evade the law in both Michigan and Pennsylvania, where it was assumed that he spent most of his time. Both states conducted extensive manhunts for the fugitive to no avail.

On September 13, 1928, a Cleveland, Ohio, grocery clerk named John Zavwroski noticed two men eating in a downtown restaurant as he walked by. One of the men looked strangely familiar to him. Zavwroski stopped and stared in the window of the restaurant. Suddenly, he recognized the stranger as Paul Poluszynski aka Jaworski. As a boy, Paul had sung in the choir of a small Ukrainian church in Butler, Pennsylvania. Zavwroski had been the choir director. He had been following Jaworski's crime career in the papers and was shocked to come face to face with the outlaw, whom he hadn't seen since both of them had been boys. Zavwroski had been a theology student but had to abandon his studies to go to Cleveland to find work. The thought of the thousands of dollars in reward money flashed through his mind. With the reward money, he could finish his studies. Zavwroski ran to a nearby telephone and notified the Cleveland Police of Jaworski's presence.

Patrolman Anthony Wieczorek and Patrolman George Effinger were dispatched to the restaurant to check on the telephone tip. As the officers walked into the restaurant and approached the two suspects, one of the men jumped to his feet and opened fire with a pistol. The gunman was later identified as Paul Jaworski. Officer Wieczorek was hit and killed instantly in the first burst of gunfire. Effinger also fell, badly wounded, under the hail of lead. Customers in the crowded restaurant threw themselves on the floor or hid under tables at the first shots. Jaworski and his lunch companion scrambled out the back door of the restaurant into an alley. Jaworski ran in one direction and his unidentified associate in another. In the midst of the confusion, Jaworski's colleague escaped. Two other Cleveland patrolmen arrived on the scene and chased Jaworski down an alley.

A bystander to the unfolding events named Ben Majsterek was wounded in the gun battle while standing in front of his nearby cigar store. Jaworski ran into an apartment building and up the stairs to the second floor. He threw open a window and jumped to the roof of an adjoining building. In the interim, a general alarm had been sounded and members of the Cleveland police force surrounded the building, exchanging shots with Jaworski. A crowd estimated to have been at least 500 people watched the gun battle. Under withering gunfire from the Cleveland police, Jaworski jumped from the roof back into the apartment house, eventually barricading himself in a first-floor kitchen. Hundreds of shots were fired into the apartment building.

Finally, the police began to fire tear gas into the flat. They fired five tear gas shells before forcing Jaworski out into the open. Suddenly, the bandit burst out of the door of the apartment building, a pistol blazing in each hand. A shotgun blast brought him down. Jaworski was wounded five times in his gunfight with the Cleveland police. The shotgun charge hit Jaworski in the side of the head. A revolver bullet also struck him in the left side of the chest just above the heart. He had two other slight wounds. The shotgun blast that struck Jaworski destroyed a group of nerve centers near the brain, which left him partially paralyzed on the right side of his body. His condition at first appeared to be serious, but by his second day in the hospital he seemed to be considerably improved. Patrolman George Effinger and Ben Majsterek, the bystander who was accidentally wounded in the gunfire, were reported to be in serious condition.

Jaworski began talking to police. He boasted that during his career of crime, he killed at least 26 men. At first he denied taking part in the *News* holdup, but confessed to the Brinks car robbery at the Ainsworth Manufacturing Company in Detroit in 1925. Jaworski also stated that he had taken another member of the gang for a "ride" shortly after the Ainsworth holdup. He shot Jimmy Wright because he had informed the police of the whereabouts of one of Jaworski's close friends. Wright's body was found on a little-frequented road in rural Farmington, Michigan, on November 22, 1925.

On September 14, 1928, Jaworski was indicted in Cleveland by a Cuyahoga County Grand Jury for the slaying of Patrolman Anthony Wieczorek. Jaworski remained completely surrounded in his Cleveland City Hospital ward by a heavy police guard. Law-enforcement officials believed that the Jaworski Gang would try to free their leader. Jaworski had been poorly dressed when he was captured by the Cleveland police. He explained to the officers that, despite the fact that he had made a quarter of a million dollars in his long career as a bank robber, he had spent all of his ill-gained wealth.

The bandit told the police that the man who escaped when he was captured was John Vassbinder. Jaworski claimed that he and Vassbinder had been working together since they both shot their way out of the Allegheny County Jail in Pittsburgh in August of 1927. He told police that they had been living at the exclusive Hotel Cleveland for several months. Jaworski later gave police the address of his actual hideout, which was located in Lakewood, Ohio, a suburb of Cleveland. At the Lakewood address, officers found a strong arsenal that included automatic shotguns, a machine gun, pistols, and a large store of ammunition.

Cleveland officers sent the weapons found in the Lakewood, Ohio, address to the Detroit Police Laboratory. A ballistics test was performed on an automatic rifle that had been found in the Jaworski hideout. Shells ejected by the automatic rifle during the test bore the same markings as some of the shells found in front of the *Detroit News* building on the day of the holdup. Presented with the results of the ballistics test, Jaworski confessed to the *Detroit News* robbery. He also stated that he was one of the two bandits who fatally wounded Sergeant George Barstad, as they were running out of the *Detroit News* building.

Jaworski also named Harry Watson and Frank "Whitey" Kraft as two of the five men who had held up the business offices of the *Detroit News*. Both Kraft and Watson had Detroit police records. Jaworski refused to say whether Frank Wallace, a friend of Watson's, had also participated in the *News* job. Wallace aka Gustin was being held in Boston at that time. According to the Wayne County Prosecutor's Office, Wallace was known to have worked with Harry Watson. Frankie Wallace was one of the leaders of the Gustin Gang of Boston, Massachusetts. The Gustin outfit was one of the predominantly Irish Mobs that ruled the Boston underworld before 1930.

Jaworski identified a house on Littlefield Avenue in Detroit as the place where the gang had divided up the loot taken from the *Detroit News*. This was only a short distance from where the gang had abandoned the stolen car used in the robbery. He also confessed that Frank "Whitey" Kraft had been the man with him in the Cleveland restaurant on the day he was captured. Both Kraft and Watson were being sought at that time by Detroit police. Persons living in the vicinity of the Jaworski Gang's Littlefield address told detectives that they had seen two men who were later identified as Jaworski and Kraft on the morning of June 6, 1928. Both men were carrying red paper bags. The red paper was used to wrap a box containing shotguns that were used in the *Detroit News* robbery. Ironically, Jaworski later claimed that he had lost his share of the *Detroit News* holdup loot in a poker game to accomplice Harry Watson the same day the robbery had occurred.

On October 20, 1928, Jaworski began the trip back to Pittsburgh. He had been extradited to Pennsylvania by Ohio authorities for execution of the death sentence that he had been waiting to complete when he broke out of the Allegheny County Jail in 1927. The Cleveland, Ohio, Prosecutor's Office ran into legal difficulties in the prosecution of

Jaworski for the murder of Patrolman Wieczorek. They thought it would be more expedient to send Jaworski back to a jurisdiction in which a death sentence was pending.

Upon arriving in Pittsburgh, Jaworski had 90 days to appeal his case to the State Supreme Court. His lawyers filed a motion for a new trial, which was promptly refused by a Pittsburgh judge. Jaworski was brought from Cleveland under heavy police guard, even though he was partially paralyzed. On his arrival in Pittsburgh, he had to be carried into the courtroom in a straight-back chair. His paralysis made it extremely difficult for Jaworski to walk. He told the judge that he would not appeal his case if the Allegheny County Court would not allow him to have a new trial.

The Jaworski execution was scheduled for 7 a.m., January 21, 1929, in the death house of the Rockview Penitentiary at Bellefonte, Pennsylvania. His attorney's attempts at getting a commutation of the death sentence and a last-minute stay of execution had all failed. In the long hours before the execution, Jaworski gave no sign of a break in his nerve. At 7 a.m. on January 21, 1929, Paul Poluszynski aka Paul Jaworski was brought into the death chamber at the Rockview Prison supported by two guards. Jaworski entered the death chamber chewing on a stogie, one of a number of cigars that he remarked on the way to the death house "must last me all my life." At the door of the death chamber, the cigar was removed from his mouth. He refused any attempts at religious consultation. When asked why by prison officials, he replied, "Aw, I used to talk against that stuff on a soap box. I want to die just like I lived." At 7:02 a.m., Jaworski was strapped into the electric chair and current was applied. At 7:06 a.m., Paul Jaworski was officially pronounced dead.

In the end, he was officially considered to have been the murderer of six people and not the 26 he had once boasted of killing. Jaworski at one point had told police officials that he had killed John Vassbinder because he was a dope addict. Shortly before he was executed, Jaworski told police that he hadn't seen Vassbinder since the two men had broken out of jail together.

The Jaworski family never claimed the body. Paul Jaworski was buried in a potter's field near Rockview Penitentiary. Shortly before he was executed, Deputy Warden William MacFarland asked Jaworski how much money he had left. "There ain't none," replied Jaworski. "It's all gone. Easy come, easy go!"

The Jaworski/Flathead Mob was responsible for a long series of depredations over a period of approximately six years that included:

• 1923—The holdup of the Detroit Savings Bank Branch in Detroit: $30,000 taken

• December 23, 1923—Holdup of a coal company paymaster at Beadling, Pennsylvania: $23,000 taken and paymaster killed

• May 17, 1924—Holdup of the Detroit Bank Branch at West Fort Street and West End in Detroit: $40,000 taken

• December 1924—Holdup of a coal company paymaster at Mt. Lebanon, Pennsylvania: guard killed, unknown amount taken

• April 14, 1925—Holdup of the American State Bank Branch in Detroit: Charles J. Taggert Jr., a young teller is killed, unknown amount taken

- April 30, 1925—Saloon holdup at Sharpsburg, Pennsylvania: unknown amount taken
- June 5, 1925—Attempted holdup of the Peninsular State Bank in Detroit
- June 13, 1925—Holdup of the Central Savings Bank in Detroit: $27,000 taken and a police officer killed
- August 8, 1925—Holdup of Henry Velick, a scrap-iron dealer at Detroit: $1,500 taken
- November 20, 1925—Holdup of a Brinks armored car taking a payroll to the Ainsworth Manufacturing Company in Detroit: $18,000 taken and a guard killed
- December 24, 1925—Holdup of a payroll of the Pittsburgh Terminal Coal Company at Mollenauer, Pennsylvania: $48,000 taken and a guard killed
- March 11, 1927—Dynamiting of an armored car owned by the Pittsburgh Terminal Coal Company at Coverdale, Pennsylvania: $104,000 taken and a guard killed
- August 18, 1927—After being convicted of murder and sentenced to die in the electric chair, Jaworski and another man shot their way out of the Allegheny County Jail at Pittsburgh and escaped; a guard is killed
- September 29, 1927—Holdup of the offices of the General Baking Company at Detroit: $5,000 taken
- June 6, 1928—Holdup of the business offices of the *Detroit News*: $25,000 taken and a patrolman killed

• • •

On the night of November 24, 1925, a group of bandits descended on the village of Cassopolis,

Michigan. Cassopolis is located in the southern part of the state about 100 miles southwest of Detroit. The outlaws had plans to rob the First National Bank of Cassopolis and came prepared to do whatever was necessary to get the vault opened. The Cassopolis job had been well planned. At about 2:30 a.m., the gang entered the town. Their first job was to round up anybody who was up and about. The village had two all-night restaurants, since it was located along highway M-60, a popular truck route to Chicago. The bandits made their first stop at the restaurant owned by Pat Wallace. Wallace was alone in the building when three of the thugs entered his place and produced pistols. Wallace was ordered to put his hands behind his back and was quickly tied up. He was marched across the street at gunpoint to another all-night diner. There they found three men including a Cass County Deputy Sheriff named Clyde Benham. These men were also tied up and taken out of the diner. While the local townspeople who were awake were rounded up, other members of the gang were busy prying open the front door to the bank. When the door was broken down, all four of the gang's prisoners were walked down to the bank and seated in a cloakroom inside the building, where they were tied to their chairs. The gangsters then set to work on the vault door. The prisoners were told to keep their heads down, since there was going to be a little blasting. Several members of the gang remained on guard outside the bank with pistols and shotguns. Using sledge hammers, the gang had first broken out a hole in the brick wall surrounding the safe. Finding that the vault was steel lined, they went to work on the heavy door. The joints of the door were "soaped" (sealed by rubbing soap into the joints) and a charge of nitroglycerin was put in and exploded. After several charges were exploded, the main vault door was blasted off. The vault was found to have a second inner door as an extra security measure. Two more charges were placed in an attempt to blast off this additional obstacle. Failing to get the safe's inner door open, the bandits fled, taking several hundred dollars in postage stamps from desks they had ransacked in the bank offices. The postage stamps were the gang's only loot for a whole night's work. The prisoners eventually freed themselves and walked out of the partially destroyed bank building unharmed.

Before the gang had taken hostages that night and attempted to rob the Cassopolis Bank, they cut the telephone cables in the front and rear of the village telephone office building. This had effectively cut the town off from the outside world. The local operator on duty that night eventually found that the bandits had missed one wire leading to Dowagiac, Michigan, a nearby hamlet approximately seven miles north of Cassopolis. Through this line, an alarm was eventually put out.

The repeated explosions at the bank awoke the whole village, and several of the town's braver souls set out to investigate the disturbance. Dr. James Kelsey, who was president of the village and the town doctor, lived in a flat over his office. The building was situated across the street from the bank. As the doctor left the building and walked toward the county jail, he was ordered to halt by the bandits who were standing in front of the bank. The doctor ignored the order and kept on walking. He ducked behind a building, where he watched one of the bandits later identified as Steven Raczkowski blowing out street lamps in the vicinity of the bank with a shotgun. Kelsey pulled out a Lugar pistol he was carrying and fired in the direction of the bank. His shot was returned by a barrage from a rifle and several shotguns. He scrambled for cover near the jail, where he found the Cass County Sheriff, Earl Sill, hiding in the dark. The sheriff, armed with only a .38 caliber revolver, felt that he was no match for the fire power of the bandits. Another man named George Jones came running out of his house in the direction of the bank. Several blasts from one of the gangsters' shotguns knocked Jones to the ground. Jones was slightly wounded as a pellet had penetrated his neck. Regaining his nerve, he picked himself up and ran home. The president of the Cassopolis Bank, Dr. J.B. Bonine, made the mistake of driving by the front of the bank and stopping his car. Blasts from several shotguns shattered the running board and body of the vehicle. The banker quickly drove home. The village druggist made a vain attempt to get a shotgun that he kept downstairs in his store. As he turned on the light and descended the stairs, a shotgun blast blew out the plate glass window and lights of his shop. The buildings near the bank were riddled with bullet and buckshot holes. Windows and doors in the immediate vicinity were in a shambles. The interior of the bank had been completely destroyed by the bandits in their attempts to blast open the safe. The gunmen kept up a steady bombardment of rifle, pistol, and shotgun fire during the time they controlled the village. The bandits fired at anything that moved or anyone who turned on a light.

Shortly after the bandits fled, officers from surrounding towns began arriving. Roadblocks were set up, and the area was scoured for the gang, but they had disappeared. The exact number of men involved in the holdup was estimated to be between five and 10. The gangsters had been careful not to kill any of the people of the town, generally shooting wide of their targets.

The Cassopolis bank job was to be the last major robbery attempted by the Kozak/Carson Mob of Detroit. It also proved to be the debut of Chester Tutha into the Detroit underworld. Tutha at that time was a 16-year-old petty thief from Hamtramck, Michigan, who had befriended some of the older gangsters in the Kozak Mob. It was Tutha's first involvement in a big-time bank robbery.

An investigation was immediately launched by the Michigan State Police in coordination with the Detroit Police Department. The gunmen, who were all Detroiters, had failed to wear masks during the forced occupation of Cassopolis, probably assuming they could never be identified by the local people. Detective Fred G. Armstrong of the Michigan State Police showed some mug shots to the men who were held prisoner during the holdup attempt. An ex-convict named Clarence Madden was picked out of the photographs and identified as one of the gunmen. Madden was a member of the Kozak Mob who lived in Lansing, Michigan. At approximately the same time that Madden was identified at Cassopolis as one of the bandits, an informer tipped off the Lansing, Michigan, police about Madden.

According to the anonymous caller, Madden and other members of the Kozak Gang were to meet at Madden's Lansing address to plan the robbery of a local bank. Police were given the time and date that the meeting was supposed to take place. At the given time, members of the Michigan State Police and Lansing Police Department raided Madden's house but found only Madden and his wife at the location. Madden was questioned and released. Lansing police posted men to follow the gangster, and the Detroit police were notified. During this time, the Detroit police were watching a house at 525 East Elizabeth in Detroit. Their information had also been based on an anonymous tip. The day after Madden's home had been raided in Lansing, Madden, his wife, and another member of the gang named James Allen made a trip to Detroit. They were observed pulling up in front of the East Elizabeth Street address. All three of the suspects went into the building. A short time later, they returned to their car in the company of Chester Tutha, Steven Raczkowski, Sam Bokosky, and Joe Konon. All of these men were known associates of the Kozak Gang.

The six men and the woman were immediately arrested by Detroit police officers. All of the men had Detroit Police Department records. According to a State Police report, Bokosky was carrying a .38 caliber pistol at the time of his arrest. A .32 caliber pistol was also found in 525 East Elizabeth, which turned out to be Chester Tutha's apartment. According to another newspaper account, all of the men were found to be carrying pistols when they were searched. The six men were taken to police headquarters and held for investigation of armed robbery. The woman was held for investigation and later released. All were considered suspects in the Cassopolis robbery.

On December 12, 1925, Clyde Benham, a Cass County deputy sheriff, positively identified Allen,

Madden, and Raczkowski as the men who had surprised him in a Cassopolis restaurant the night of November 24, 1925. Benham was one of the four men the gang had taken prisoner before they tried to rob the bank.

Mrs. E.C. Dunning, who lived in a flat directly above the Cassopolis Bank, later told State Police investigators that two men who were later identified as Chester Tutha and Joe Konon had come to her flat. This incident occurred several days before the Cassopolis bank robbery. The two strangers had asked Mrs. Dunning if there was a stenographer in the building. She told them no, and they departed. On December 13, 1925, she picked Tutha and Konon out of a lineup at Detroit police headquarters. The two men were taken back to Cassopolis and held at the Cass County Jail where they were charged with "robbing a bank in the night time." Konon and Tutha were arraigned on this charge on December 19, 1925. Examination was planned for January 11, 1926, but was postponed until February 8, 1926. Tutha, Konon, Madden, and Allen were bound over for trial at Cassopolis by the Circuit Court. Raczkowski was later discharged and turned over to the Detroit police for a D.S.R. car barn holdup.

On January 9, 1926, Detective Armstrong of the Michigan State Police arrested another suspect in the Cassopolis job. Alex Hanacki was picked up coming out of a Detroit restaurant. Hanacki was associated with the Kozak Gang. He later confessed to Assistant Wayne County Prosecutor James E. Chenot that he had been involved in at least a dozen holdups in Detroit during the previous year. He named Konon and Tutha as two of the six men who held up the Cassopolis, Michigan, bank. Hanacki was held on a charge of armed robbery. While these events were unfolding, the recognized leaders of the Kozak Gang were being sought by police on a first-degree murder charge. On January 11, 1926, Patrolman Andrew Rusinko was shot down by two gunmen who were attempting to hold up a jitney driver at Six Mile and Woodward in Detroit.

Sometimes referred to as a modern-day "James Gang," the Kozak Mob terrorized southeastern Michigan for almost a year, before the destruction of the gang after the Cassopolis job. The gang was named for Phillip "Russian Shorty" Kozak. Kozak, who stood 5'2" tall, more than made up for his size in ferocity. Born in the village of Pienski, Russia, in 1896, the pint-sized gunman had immigrated to the U.S. around 1914. After working as a day laborer for several years, Kozak decided that there were easier ways to make a buck. He began his criminal career actually involved in the process of making money. He was arrested by federal officers and later convicted as a counterfeiter. He served 18 months in the federal penitentiary at Atlanta, Georgia.

Known in the Detroit underworld as a triggerman, Detroit police believed that Phillip Kozak's chief value to the gang was his brutal temper and ability with a gun. The true leader of the Kozak outfit and the man given credit by police for the gang's early success was James "Jimmy" Carson. Jimmy Carson was born in Chicago, Illinois, in 1896; Carson's parents had originally immigrated from Denmark. Carson was arrested in Ohio for bank robbery when he was in his teens. He was tried and convicted of bank robbery and served four years in the Ohio state-prison system. After his release, he moved to Detroit, where he planned to go straight and get a job. He found employment on a Great Lakes freighter as a merchant marine. Carson stayed on the boats for a short time. Tired of life as a sailor, he returned to Detroit and worked at various jobs. Carson eventually decided that his financial progress was too slow. He began holding up grocery stores and filling stations to supplement his income. His success at eluding the police soon attracted other underworld characters to Carson.

The charismatic Carson became the leader of a gang of safecrackers and gunmen that included Phillip Kozak, Clarence Madden, James Allen, Chester Tutha, Joseph Konon, Steven Raczkowski, Alex Hanacki, and Frank Dion alias Frank Clark. It was conservatively estimated that the gang was involved in at least 100 holdups during a period of approximately 12 months. Carson claimed that in one night on his way from Detroit to Ann Arbor, he held up eight oil stations to supply himself with what he called "chicken feed."

The gang specialized in holding up banks, grocery stores, filling stations, and drugstores. Operating in similar fashion to Detroit's earlier Shotgun Gang, the bandits would commit their holdups and then scatter to various rural hideouts. They eventually made their headquarters on a farm at Ridgeway, Michigan, in Lenawee County, about 60 miles south of Detroit. The farm was owned by John Barlow. From this location, the gang regularly committed robberies in Detroit, Ann Arbor, Ypsilanti, Milan, Saline, and other towns and villages in southern Michigan. Barlow's daughter, Miss Irene Walling Smith, was a girlfriend of Carson and later Dion.

After the arrest of most of the gang as a result of

the Cassopolis holdup, Kozak and Carson decided they needed some money. They planned another bank robbery, but decided that it would first be necessary to steal a car that they could use for the heist. On January 11, 1926, Kozak and Carson boarded a jitney in front of the Ford Motor Company Plant in Highland Park, Michigan. They rode in the vehicle to the corner of Six Mile Road and Woodward Avenue in Detroit. The jitney driver stopped to let out the only other passenger besides the two thugs, a young woman. Once the woman got out and disappeared around a corner, Kozak and Carson both pulled guns in an attempt to rob the driver and hijack his vehicle. Ordered to get out of the jitney, the driver put up a fight, and one of the bandits hit him in the head with the butt of a pistol and pushed him out of the vehicle. The commotion attracted the attention of a Detroit police officer named Andrew Rusinko. Rusinko had just walked out of a nearby bank. Observing the robbery in progress, he ran towards the jitney. Both Carson and Kozak fired at the officer, killing him instantly. The two gunmen escaped in the jitney that was found by Detroit police later the same day wrecked in Detroit. With a combined effort of the Detroit, Hamtramck, and State Police departments, a manhunt began. Detectives of the Detroit Police Department later received an underworld tip that Kozak and a man named Jimmy killed Rusinko.

At 1 a.m. on January 16, 1926, Detective John Mickley of the Hamtramck police spotted Kozak and another man, later identified as Carson, coming out of a Hamtramck restaurant on Joseph Campau Avenue. Mickley had arrested Kozak on three previous occasions and knew the gunman well. As

Mickley approached the two men and started to reach for his pistol, Kozak grabbed hold of his arm and asked, "What's the matter, Mickley?" Mickley jerked away, and Carson shot him several times in the back. Kozak and Carson fled, leaving Mickley lying on the sidewalk. Although he was in serious condition, Mickley would eventually recover.

Later the same evening, Carson and Kozak suspected that they were being followed by a Detroit police patrolman. Officer Edward Gerdes had been on his way home when Carson fired at the patrolman. The bullet ricocheted off his badge and hit Gerdes in the hand. At 3 a.m. on the morning of January 16, 1926, Detroit police received a tip that a man fitting Carson's description had used a public phone in Hamtramck to call a garage in Ridgeway, Michigan. A group of Detroit, Hamtramck, and Michigan State Police officers accompanied by Washtenaw County deputy sheriffs drove out to Ridgeway at 9 a.m. that morning. The officers made inquiries around the village, and by 9 p.m., January 16, they had located the Barlow farm, which the gang was using as a base of operations.

Police surrounded the house and outbuildings. However, Kozak and Carson, who were hiding in a barn, managed to escape the dragnet. Carson was able to get a ride back to Detroit later the same evening, while Kozak hid in a Ridgeway, Michigan, garage. On Sunday, January 17, 1926, Kozak was arrested in Ridgeway and returned to Detroit. He denied having anything to do with the Rusinko shooting but admitted that he had been present the night that Detective Mickley had been shot. He also implicated fellow gang member Frank Dion. The day the police raided the Barlow farm they found a telegram from Barlow's daughter, Irene Smith. Miss Smith had been visiting Dion's parents and had accompanied the gangster to Montreal, Canada. The telegram, which was sent to her father, stated that she would arrive in Detroit by train the following Monday. Montreal police were wired, and Dion was picked up and returned to Detroit. A week before Kozak was apprehended in Ridgeway, a warrant had been issued for his arrest as a suspect in the Cassopolis, Michigan, robbery. This warrant was the result of statements made to police by Alex Hanacki implicating Kozak. Kozak later admitted that he was present at Cassopolis the night the gang attempted to rob the bank.

On January 19, 1926, Kozak confessed to Assistant Wayne County Prosecutor James E. Chenot that he was present when Officer Andrew Rusinko was killed but refused to name who shot the officer. Kozak also confessed to a number of other robberies, both in Michigan and out of state. He told police that Frank Dion had been with him the night that Rusinko was shot. When faced with a first-degree murder charge, Dion began to talk. He denied being present or having anything to do with the Rusinko shooting. He readily confessed to participating in 15 holdups in the Detroit area. He also admitted that he had been with several members of the gang when they held up a D.S.R. streetcar barn in Detroit on November 29, 1925. Both Dion and Kozak later pled guilty to the D.S.R. holdup. On February 3, 1926, they were sentenced in Detroit Recorders Court to 15 to 30 years with 20 recommended in Marquette Prison.

James Carson was still being sought by police.

His sometime girlfriend, Irene Walling Smith, was picked up by Detroit police for investigation. Through the efforts of detectives, Miss Smith was persuaded to call Carson and arrange to meet him in Detroit. Smith had known Carson's whereabouts all along but had steadfastly refused to tell police anything. When she finally agreed to set up the meeting, she told officers, "I wouldn't help you against him if he had stuck to holdups, but when he began to shoot people he was done for, as far as I was concerned. He told me once he would never shoot a man to kill."

Smith called Carson and arranged a meeting for 7 p.m., February 7, 1926, in Detroit. At 7:20 p.m., Carson was surrounded by Detroit and Michigan State Police. He surrendered without a fight. Carson had roughly disguised himself by growing a mustache and dyeing his hair, mustache, and eyebrows black. He was poorly dressed in an old brown sweater, old trousers, and he wore rubbers on his shoes. He had smeared his face with coal dust.

On February 9, 1926, both Carson and Kozak made joint confessions that they had both shot Rusinko. Kozak finally admitted to pulling the trigger. Carson claimed that he had fired the first shot at Rusinko, and Kozak had fired afterward. It was determined that either wound could have killed the police officer.

Kozak was sent to Marquette Prison on his robbery conviction. On December 14, 1928, he was discharged from Ionia State Hospital for deportation to Poland. Carson was convicted of first-degree murder in the slaying of Detroit Police Officer Andrew Rusinko and sentenced to life in prison.

A total of eight members of the Kozak Gang were

tried on various charges:

**James Allen** and **Clarence Madden** were tried in Cass County Circuit Court for the November 24, 1925, Cassopolis robbery. Both men were found not guilty.

**Joe Konon** was tried and convicted in Detroit Recorders Court for the November 29, 1925, robbery of a D.S.R. car barn in Detroit. He was sentenced to 5-15 years in Jackson Prison.

**Steven Raczkowski** was tried and convicted in Detroit Recorders Court for the November 29, 1925, robbery of the D.S.R. car barn in Detroit and sentenced to 15-30 years in Marquette Prison.

**Frank Dion aka Clark** was tried and convicted in Detroit Recorders Court for the November 29, 1925, robbery of the D.S.R. car barn in Detroit and sentenced to 15-30 years in Marquette Prison.

**Phillip Kozak** was tried and convicted in Detroit Recorders Court for the November 29, 1925, robbery of the D.S.R. car barn and sentenced to 15-30 years in Marquette Prison.

**James Carson** pled guilty to the murder of Detroit Police Officer Andrew Rusinko on January 11, 1926, and was given a life sentence.

Chester Tutha and Joe Konon were returned to the custody of Detroit officers on February 21, 1926. Residents of Cassopolis had been unable to identify either of the two men as being the bandits who attempted to rob the town bank. Upon their return to Detroit, they were both immediately charged with a December 5, 1925, holdup of the Michigan Savings Bank, in which $808 had been taken. Both men were later released on this charge. Konon was later convicted of another robbery. The Cassopolis robbery was the beginning of the end for the Kozak Gang. Somehow Chester Tutha managed to evade prosecution on the various charges that were thrown at him. In so doing, he had gained a reputation as a safecracker and a stickup man in the Detroit underworld.

On the morning of April 2, 1927, four men walked into the shoe store of Abe Hallmeyer at 10232 Grand River Avenue in Detroit. Three of the men sat down and were fitted with shoes. A fourth man stood by the door. Suddenly, all four men pulled guns. One hundred dollars was taken from the cash register, a ring was taken from Hallmeyer's nephew, and another customer was robbed of $10. One of the holdup men walked out of the store wearing a new pair of shoes. Hallmeyer called the police.

Less than 10 minutes after the shoe store holdup, two men fitting the description given by Hallmeyer were spotted by police. A detachment of detectives from the Bethune Station noticed the men sitting in a Hudson Coach auto at Poe and Bethune Streets. As the officers approached the car on foot, both men attempted to pull guns. They were quickly overpowered and placed under arrest. The two suspects gave their names as Chester Tutha, 18 years old, and Alfred Grabale, 19 years old. Both men were wearing new pairs of shoes with the Hallmeyer trademark. Several boxes of new shoes that had been taken from the store were found in the car. The two men were taken to Detroit police headquarters, where they were identified by both

Hallmeyer and the owner of a Detroit clothing store that had recently been robbed. Another man who worked as a filling-station attendant also identified Tutha and Grabale as the bandits that had robbed him of $70. This station and three others were all robbed the same day within a period of seven minutes. Both Tutha and Grabale were held on a charge of armed robbery. On the second day of their trial in May of 1927, both men pled guilty in Detroit Recorders Court to the charges. They were sentenced to serve 7½ to 15 years in Jackson Prison. It was Tutha's first conviction.

Tutha made important underworld contacts while serving his first hitch in state prison. His previous association with the Kozak Mob no doubt enhanced his reputation as a safecracker and gunman. He served almost five years of his original sentence and was paroled to Detroit on November 24, 1931.

Shortly after Tutha was released from prison, he was arrested in the company of a tinsmith named Joe Sceatko. Tutha was arrested for investigation, and Sceatko was held as a suspect in the gun-smuggling plot that led to the August 27, 1931, attempted jailbreak at Marquette Prison. During the chaos, a prison doctor and a trustee were slain and four convicts had committed suicide. Information as to who was responsible for the smuggling had been obtained from a well-known Detroit and Hamtramck gunman named Walter Tylczak. Upon his conviction in Detroit on an armed-robbery case, Tylczak suddenly became talkative. According to a statement by Tylczak, a Hamtramck gangster named Chester Kolodzieski was responsible for shipping the guns to "Hardrock" (underworld slang for Marquette Prison).

Tylczak claimed that every convict that was released from Marquette promised to try and ship contraband back into the prison. In Tylczak's words, "Most don't, Chester did."

Tylczak told police that the gang had hired Sceatko, who was a tinsmith, to put false bottoms in cans of whole chicken. Canned chicken was allowed to be ordered by individual inmates at Marquette Prison. According to Tylczak the guns and ammunition were put into the cans and then closed back up again. Tylczak confessed that he, Alex "Lefty" Zydowski, and Sceatko got $50 each for the job. The Detroit police claimed that shortly after the Marquette Prison trouble of August 1931, prison officials had confiscated a letter written to Zydowski from Stanley "Big Stack" Podolski, thanking him "for keeping your promise and not forgetting your pals in stir."

After this information became public, Circuit Judge Victor E. Sprague of Cheboygan, Michigan, was immediately appointed as a one-man grand jury to investigate the attempted Marquette Prison break of August 27, 1931. Sceatko was sent to Marquette to testify before the grand jury as to his role in the gun-smuggling incident. Chester Kolodziewski, who was on trial at that time for breaking parole, also named Sceatko in a confession he made to police. According to Kolodziewski, who vehemently denied any involvement in the job, Tylczak had planned the gun smuggling, and "Lefty" Zydowski drove the cans of chicken up to Marquette and hid them in thick underbrush near the prison. They were supposedly picked up and carried into the prison by a trustee who was paid off by the gang. "Big Stack" Podolski was named by both Tylczak and Zydowski as the man behind the attempted "blastout" at Marquette Prison in August of 1931.

It was suspected but never proved that Chester Tutha played a role in the gun-smuggling plot. No one was ever tried for smuggling the guns that were used in the Marquette Prison fiasco. The evidence presented to the grand jury investigating the causes of the 1931 riot at Marquette were inconclusive. Tutha would go on to become the leader of a gang of safecrackers that operated in the Detroit and Hamtramck area for many years. By the mid-'30s, Tutha would join forces with several Purple Gangsters. The Purples used Tutha and his gang for their safecracking abilities. Louis Fleisher and several Purple Gangsters would work with Tutha and his Mob in a series of rural-area robberies in which safes were removed and carted away to other locations to be opened.

# The Ferguson Grand Jury

"Dear Sirs:

It seems there is a great deal of vice going on in Detroit, and as long as the police are a part of it, it seems perhaps the government should know something about it in order to do a bit of clean up work."

—*Letter from Mrs. Janet MacDonald to the Detroit office of the F.B.I., August 5, 1939*

"It was illegal. It was unethical. But it was not grand larceny with a receiving account. In my book if an officer hijacks a racketeer that's stealing. If the racket guy brings the money in and lays it down that's not stealing. That's the way I see it."

—*Former Detroit Police Inspector Raymond W. Boettcher, Ferguson Grand Jury witness, January 4, 1944*

I t was almost noon on Saturday, July 8, 1939, when Inspector Perry Myers of the Detroit Police Department's Mounted Division left his office in back of the Bethune Street station. Myers was on his way to a nearby restaurant for lunch. As he cut across an alley that ran behind the station house between Horton and Custer Avenues, he heard the roar of an automobile engine. Myers glanced down the alley and saw a Buick sedan racing towards him. He quickly stepped back out of sight and waited. As the car slowed to a roll at Bethune Street, the inspector saw a pistol lying on the front-seat cushion. Myers pulled his own revolver and stepped up to the side of the sedan. He ordered the four startled men in the car to shut off the motor and put up their hands. As the four men climbed out of the vehicle, Myers noticed two cigar boxes and several more pistols. Both boxes were full of money. The inspector paraded the four men back to the Bethune Station with their hands in the air. It was first reported that $1,600 in cash was found in the two cigar boxes. (The exact amount was never known.) Seven hundred thirty-seven dollars was taken off the persons of the four suspects. The men were quickly identified as Joe Holtzman, Lou Jacobs, Irving Feldman, and Sidney Cooper. All four suspects were associated with a group of young thugs known as the Junior Purple Gang. These were men who were several years younger than the core group of Purples. Inspector Ray Boettcher, who worked at Bethune Station at the time, later admitted that the four Purple Gangster suspects were all well known to him. Boettcher described them as racketeers whom police suspected of shaking down legitimate businesses.

At first, there was some confusion as to what exactly was going on. "There's nothing wrong," Holtzman told detectives. "I've just got some change here for a couple of the joints, and I need the guns to guard it!" The bills found in the cigar boxes were all brand new and in unusual denominations. There were several packages of one-dollar bills. Each package contained $100 and still had bank wrappers on it. Other bills were consecutively serial numbered. To his surprise Myers discovered that the pistols he found in the suspects' car were not loaded. The four Purples explained to detectives that they had gotten the money they were carrying from Izzy Bernstein. The suspects disclaimed any knowledge of the guns found in the car.

As Bethune detectives began to question the four suspects, a robbery report was phoned in from another precinct. Why the robbery was reported to the wrong precinct remained a mystery. The offices of the Great Lakes Realty Company in the Stormfeltz/Lovely building located directly behind the Bethune Station had just been held up by two men. The bandits allegedly tied up the office manager, Dr. Martin Robinson, his wife, and a secretary, and escaped with an undetermined amount of cash. A sergeant and two patrolmen were sent to the offices of the Great Lakes Realty Co. to investigate the robbery complaint. When the officers arrived, Dr. Robinson and his staff confirmed that they had been robbed. Dr. Robinson was a 1914 graduate of the University of Michigan Medical School. He had only practiced medicine briefly. He later owned and operated a drugstore and dabbled in Michigan politics. At one time, Robinson had even run for Detroit City Council and was also rumored to be involved in the Detroit numbers racket.

Details of the robbery checked with those already noted during the questioning of the four suspects. Two of the pistols found in the suspects' car were registered to Robinson. Descriptions of the bandits, the cigar boxes, and the denominations of the bills that were stolen immediately linked the four Purple Gangsters to the robbery. Robinson and his staff were brought to the Bethune Station to view the suspects. Dr. Robinson reluctantly identified Lou Jacobs as one of the bandits, and his secretary, Florence Wolfe, identified Irving Feldman as the man who tied her up. When Robinson came face to face with the four suspects at the station house, he was reported to have turned white. He was very anxious not to file a complaint even though he had tentatively identified one of the men, and his secretary had pointed out another. Detectives refused to let Robinson drop the armed-robbery charge, and the four Purples were locked up.

Two days after the reported holdup, Robinson was again asked by detectives to come to police headquarters to view the four suspects in a lineup. This time Robinson told detectives that he could not identify any of the men, and he was positive that these were not the men who had robbed him. It was obvious that there was something very peculiar about the Robinson case. For some reason, Robinson seemed to be trying to cover up the robbery. After he learned that Robinson had first identified and then refused to identify the suspects in the case, Fred Frahm, Superintendant of the Detroit police, had ordered a police investigation of the Robinson case. The case was officially assigned to Bethune Station Detectives Wilfred E. Brouillet and Byron E. Farrish.

Coincidentally, as this drama was unfolding, Lt. John McCarthy of the Racket Squad and his men raided the Square Deal policy house in Detroit. A man who worked at the place claimed it was owned by somebody named Robinson. When Frahm questioned Robinson about his connection to this numbers operation, Robinson replied, "Well, you know,

Superintendent, I like to help people. I know this man, yes. I knew he needed some money, and I loaned him some. That's the only interest I have in the place."

"What about the Great Lakes and those other policy joints?" asked Frahm.

"The same with them," Robinson replied. "I like to help people out. They need money, and I lend it to them. I am always willing to help. I don't have any other interest in the places."

The day after the Square Deal policy house was raided, Lt. McCarthy and his men raided a handbook operated by Sammy Millman (younger brother of Harry). Police had received information that Millman had threatened Robinson not to identify any of the robbery suspects.

On July 11, after much police coercion, Robinson again positively identified Lou Jacobs as one of the holdup men. Throughout the whole identification process, the doctor continued to be very reluctant to identify any of the suspects. "Can't we just call this whole thing off?" Robinson asked reporters as he left police headquarters.

On July 20, 1939, the four armed-robbery suspects were examined before Judge John V. Brennan in Detroit Recorders Court. Once again, Dr. Robinson failed to make a positive identification of any of the men. Undaunted by the reluctant Robinson, the judge held all four men for trial on charges of armed robbery.

The strange circumstances surrounding the Robinson holdup case would eventually be brought to light during the January 1940 trial of the four suspects. For all practical purposes, however, the Robinson case would remain an ordinary robbery investigation until early in 1940. Nobody could foresee in July of 1939 that this seemingly insignificant case would bring about revelations that would mark the beginning of the end for large-scale underworld gambling operations in Detroit and the surrounding area. Possibly this case would never have gotten any public attention had it not been for a startling chain of events that was set into motion in August of 1939.

• • •

On the evening of August 5, 1939, Mrs. Janet MacDonald dressed herself and her 11-year-old daughter Pearl in their best outfits. She then took her daughter by the hand, and they left the boarding house in which they lived. The mother and daughter walked to a nearby garage that Mrs. MacDonald had rented several weeks earlier. Inside the garage, she had carefully prepared her car for a final journey. A hose was connected to the exhaust pipe and fed into the vehicle through a hole that had been broken in the rear window of the car. Lying on the back seat of the sedan were two neatly tied stacks of letters. The letters were addressed to Michigan Governor Dickinson, the three daily Detroit newspapers, John S. Bugas, Special Agent in charge of the Detroit office of the F.B.I., and Police Commissioner Heindrich Pickert. Mrs. MacDonald had already posted copies of these letters earlier that day, but she wanted to be thorough. Closing the garage door behind them, she started the car and with her daughter sitting next to her on the front seat, they quietly slipped into eternity. The bodies of Mrs. MacDonald and her daughter Pearl were not found until 8 p.m. the following evening by the owner of the garage. The body of Mrs. MacDonald was slumped over in the front seat, and the child's body was found on the floor.

Janet MacDonald, 36, had killed herself and her daughter as the result of unrequited love for a small-time Detroit numbers racketeer named William McBride. McBride had been the manager of the Great Lakes policy house, an illegal numbers betting operation located in Detroit, where Janet MacDonald worked as a bookkeeper. Accusations in the letters MacDonald had left behind tied certain members of the Detroit Police Department to the local underworld gambling industry through graft protection payoffs. According to the letters left by Mrs. MacDonald, McBride had been in charge of the graft payments made to Detroit police for protection. She named Lt. John McCarthy as one of the officers who received a substantial monthly protection payment. Ironically known as "Honest John," McCarthy was in charge of the Detroit Police Department's Racket Squad and had been involved in the Robinson hold-up case. She also claimed that McBride made monthly payments to a large number of sergeants and patrolmen whom she did not name. In her letters, Mrs. MacDonald claimed to know a great deal about the policy and bookmaking rackets in Detroit and stated that other high-ranking police officials besides McCarthy were also on the gamblers' payroll.

When William McBride read about the suicide of his former lover and her daughter in the morning papers, he caught a cab and had the driver take him to Toledo, Ohio. McBride spent the night in various Toledo beer gardens. The following day he began to hitchhike back to Detroit. By this time, Detroit police wanted very badly to talk to McBride, and a warrant had been issued for his arrest. McBride was picked up by Michigan State Police in a drunken stupor. He was rushed back to Detroit police head-quarters where the gambler was grilled for more than 10 hours by detectives.

McBride described himself as a small-time racket guy lucky to make $48 a week. He told police that he had bootlegged during Prohibition, tended bar, and later worked as a "capper" at various hand-books around Detroit for $5 a day. McBride claimed he had met Lou Synder, the owner of the Great Lakes policy house, 10 years earlier. Synder later offered McBride a job at the numbers joint, and he eventually worked his way up to manager of the operation.

According to McBride, he had met Janet MacDonald in a downtown Detroit beer garden known as the Cowshed three years before. He began to date Janet and later got her a job at the policy house as a typist. McBride told police that he was divorced and that his ex-wife and 10-year-old son lived in Sandusky, Ohio. "Aren't you the payoff man for the policy house?" McBride was asked by a detective. "No, I'm not. Not me. I've been a bartender, a bootlegger, and I've never given a policeman so much as a cigar!" McBride stated that he did not know Lt. McCarthy personally. McCarthy had arrested both McBride and Janet MacDonald the previous fall in a raid on the Great Lakes policy house. McBride insisted, however, that he knew nothing about any graft payments. McBride told detectives that he had seen Janet the night she killed herself, but that he had refused to take her out because he was trying to break off his relationship with her.

All of Janet MacDonald's suicide letters consistently conflicted with McBride's story. According to the notes, McBride was the payoff man for the principal gambling interests in the city, and Lt. John McCarthy had conspired with gamblers and was on the syndicate payroll. In one letter, MacDonald stated that Lt. McCarthy always warned the gambling house of impending raids with a phone call. Officers who worked in the precinct and refused to take graft payments were demoted or transferred. McCarthy was the only Detroit police officer specifically named in Mrs. MacDonald's accusations.

McBride was distraught over the death of his lover and her young daughter. "I did not want to marry her because I was not good enough for her," he told police. "She should not have done it. She had no reason to do it!" Concerned over the serious charges in Janet MacDonald's suicide notes, Mayor Richard Reading ordered Police Superintendent Fred Frahm to make a complete investigation of the charges. McCarthy would remain on active duty pending the outcome of the inquiry.

• • •

During the time that the MacDonald suicide occurred and the police graft investigation was gaining momentum, Police Commissioner Heindrich Pickert was in California. In his absence Superintendent of Police Fred Frahm was the highest-ranking police officer in the city and in that capacity was put in charge of the inquiry. Taking a strangely relaxed approach to the investigation, Frahm promptly turned over the responsibility to conduct the investigation to Chief Inspector Fred R. Clarke. Frahm then left the city for a vacation in Wisconsin. In Frahm's absence, Clarke became acting head of the Detroit Police Department. On August 10, 1939, the police department officially announced that Lt. John McCarthy had been exonerated of all of the charges made against him in the Janet MacDonald suicide notes. The police investigation of the graft charges was beginning to look like a whitewash.

By August 11, 1939, local media reporters could not get any information whatsoever from Detroit police headquarters as to the progress of the graft investigation. A *Detroit Free Press* headline read: "Headquarters Quiet Enough to Hear Investigation Drop." Newspaper editorials began to demand for Police Commissioner Pickert's return from California to take personal charge of the apparently stalled investigation. Other journalists questioned why McCarthy had been exonerated so quickly of the serious charges against him. Mayor Richard Reading continued to insist on a hands-off attitude in regard to the police department graft investigation until Commissioner Pickert was back in the city.

After Acting Superintendent Inspector Fred Clark had cleared police officials of any wrongdoing, Assistant Prosecutor William E. Dowling had pressed on with the graft investigation practically on his own. On August 10, 1939, Wayne County Prosecutor Duncan McCrea called a halt to the investigation of the charges being conducted by the chief assistant, stating that the Wayne County Prosecutor's Office had an inadequate investigation staff with which to pursue the matter. "I am as anxious as anyone to get to the bottom of all this, but it is futile when we do not have our own investigators. All it amounts to is the police department investigating itself."

The quick termination of the prosecutor's investigation and the stand-by-and-watch attitude of Mayor Richard Reading started a public clamor for a grand jury investigation. The Detroit newspapers argued that a grand jury investigation would be the only legal vehicle that could be impartial yet thorough. Editorials noted that policy houses and other forms of illegal gambling had been operating wide open without any police interference for years. This, journalists contended, was reason enough for the public to have a suspicious attitude towards the Detroit Police Department. By the middle of August, Mayor Reading was still saying that a grand jury should only be called if Chief Inspector Clark's investigation showed a need for one.

In August of 1939, Mayor Reading changed his position and was appealing for a grand jury investigation into the rumors and charges linking certain Detroit police officials with organized underworld gambling. McCrea rejected Reading's suggestion to petition the courts for a grand jury. This, coupled with the Prosecutor's Office dropping the investigation, only added fuel to the fire. This strange change of attitude on the part of the mayor may have had a lot to do with the fact that he was up for reelection that November. On August 21, 1939, the Wayne County Circuit Court judges unanimously chose Judge Homer Ferguson to act as a one-man grand juror and appointed Chester P. O'Hara as the special prosecutor to investigate charges of police corruption.

Judge Homer Ferguson had been one of five men appointed by the late Michigan Governor Fred W. Green to fill one of the newly created circuit judgeships in Wayne County. Ferguson was born in Harrison City, Pennsylvania, in 1889. As a young man, Ferguson had worked as a public school teacher to earn money to go to law school. He eventually was appointed principal of a school in Export, Pennsylvania, before being accepted to the University of Michigan Law School, where he graduated in 1913. That same year, he opened a law practice in Detroit, where he was married and began to raise a family. Ferguson had developed a reputation for honesty throughout his legal career and had a great interest in civic affairs.

Chester O'Hara was born in Muskegon, Michigan, in 1890. He graduated from the University of Michigan Law School in 1910. At the age of 20, he was granted a special dispensation from the Michigan Supreme Court that allowed him to practice law before reaching his majority. Special Prosecutor Chester P. O'Hara had a reputation as a maverick and brought considerable experience to the grand jury both as a prosecutor and an investigator. As a young prosecutor, O'Hara had conducted the prosecution of the Detroit election recount fraud case in which 18 of 20 defendants were convicted of conspiracy in 1926. He won this case even though he had been opposed by a competent staff of 10 defense attorneys. As an Assistant Wayne County Prosecutor, O'Hara successfully convicted the President of the American Bank of Detroit and five bank officers on embezzlement charges. O'Hara was later elected Prosecutor of Berien County, Michigan, a post that he held for four years. He then served as attorney for the City of Jackson, Michigan. O'Hara had served on the staff of the Michigan Attorney General's office. In 1936, he had unsuccessfully opposed Duncan C. McCrea in the race for the Wayne County prosecutor's office. The backgrounds of

Ferguson and O'Hara combined brought many years of experience in public office to their positions as grand juror and special prosecutor.

On August 29, 1939, Racket Squad Lt. John McCarthy became the first of many witnesses to go before the Ferguson Grand Jury. After several days of testimony, McCarthy was cited for contempt of court after being caught in a lie by the special prosecutor. He was sentenced to five days in the Wayne County Jail. On August 31, 1939, McCarthy was suspended from the department by Commissioner Heindrich Pickert. In November of 1939, William McBride died in Florida from complications of pneumonia. The Ferguson Grand Jury had lost an important witness. But this was just the beginning.

· · ·

The armed-robbery trial for the four Junior Purple Gangsters was originally scheduled for November of 1939. Although the grand jury had begun calling witnesses in August, they had made little headway. The trial of the four men was adjourned several times. However, a new city administration took office on January 2, 1940. Richard Reading had lost the 1939 mayoral race to Edward Jeffries Jr. The mayor's new police commissioner, Frank D. Eaman, was eager to get to the bottom of the Robinson case and the accusations of a police graft scandal.

The four defendants were represented by Sidney Sherman, a well-known Detroit area criminal attorney. At the Recorders Court examination of Holtzman, Cooper, Feldman, and Jacobs on the charge of armed robbery, Sherman had stated that the Robinson incident was not a robbery at all. According to Sherman, Robinson had merely been conducting business transactions in gambling matters with the defendants.

Jury selection in the Dr. Martin B. Robinson holdup case began on January 9, 1940. After three previous adjournments, the case was finally assigned to Recorders Court Judge Thomas Cotter on January 11, 1940. The defense team consisted of Sidney Sherman, P.J.M. Hally, and George Fitzgerald. All three defense attorneys continued to argue that there was no holdup. During the course of the trial, Assistant Prosecutor John A. Ricca attempted to show the jury that Dr. Robinson had indeed been held up at his office by the four defendants on July 8, 1939. The defense continued to contend that the holdup was really nothing more than a gambling transaction.

When the defendants were put on the witness stand, each of them told the jury that the whole incident was faked. Robinson had owed the Purples more than $3,000 on a lost horse-racing bet. Robinson had asked them to tie him and his office staff up to make the whole thing look like a holdup. That way he could collect on his insurance and be compensated for the money he had lost. According to the defense, that was the reason that Robinson had called the robbery report in to the wrong precinct. This would allow the men time to get away. The guns that were found in the defendants' car had been given to them as collateral for the balance of the money owed. Robinson had paid the Purples $2,600 on a $3,100 bet. The four defendants' capture by police was an unforeseen quirk in the holdup-story plan. Other information obtained long after the trial from underworld sources was that the four Purples were merely shaking down Robinson for protection money. Again, according to this scenario, Robinson had asked the men to make the incident look like a holdup so he could collect on his insurance. Robinson was in the policy and numbers racket and was considered an easy target by the young thugs.

On January 12, 1940, Mrs. Senna Robinson (wife of Dr. Martin Robinson) took the witness stand. She told the court that she and the secretary, Florence Wolfe, had arrived at the offices of Great Lakes Realty when the robbery was in progress, but Mrs. Robinson had immediately fainted and remembered nothing. When Florence Wolfe took the witness stand, she positively identified Irving Feldman as one of the two bandits she saw in the office when she returned that day. Mrs. Robinson was in a state of collapse after her testimony, and a recess was called. That same day, the two detectives who were assigned to the Robinson case disappeared.

The Robinson case had been a routine armed-robbery trial until the morning of January 11, 1940. During the noon recess of the trial, Assistant Prosecutor John A. Ricca was seated at the counsel table. Detective Byron Farrish walked up to Ricca and whispered, "Do I have to tell about the $1,000 I gave back to Dr. Robinson?" Ricca was shocked. He immediately notified Chief Assistant Prosecutor William Dowling of this new development.

Police investigators were then called in and Chief of Detectives John Hoffman questioned Detectives Farrish and Brouillet. Both detectives admitted that they had returned $1,000 of the holdup money to Dr. Robinson the day of the reported holdup. They had done this on the orders of a superior officer whom they refused to identify. It was later learned that the superior officer was Inspector Myers. Detective Farrish had originally reported that $600 had been found in the bandits' car. He now claimed that there had actually been $1,600. He had originally written this amount into the evidence book. He stated that he later doctored the 1 to make it look like $600. Farrish had no right to give the evidence money back to Robinson without a court order. After several hours of questioning by Hoffman, the two detectives asked their superiors for permission to go out to get a cup of coffee. Farrish and Brouillet walked out of the building and never returned. Later that same day, Farrish phoned Chief of Detectives John Hoffman. "I know I am in the grease, and I'm not coming back," Farrish told the chief. "You better come in anyway," Hoffman replied. "Such a resignation isn't official." "I don't want to," said Farrish, "I quit." Defense counsel of the four Purple Gangster defendants immediately made a motion for a mistrial when they learned of the disappearance of the two detectives. The defense argued that the detectives' absence prevented necessary cross examination.

On January 13, 1940, the new police commissioner, Frank D. Eaman, ordered a complete investigation. One of the first police officials questioned by Eaman about the peculiar discrepancies in the Robinson case was Police Superintendent Fred Frahm. Frahm told the commissioner that Farrish told him he had returned some of the holdup money to Robinson because the doctor had needed it for a real estate deal. By disclosing this information to the police commissioner, Frahm indirectly admitted that he knew about the return of the evidence money to Dr. Robinson. Heads soon began to roll at

Detroit police headquarters. Eaman believed that there had been a coverup in the police department. The commissioner fired Superintendent Fred Frahm, who was later allowed to resign. Earlier that same day, Eaman had accepted the resignation of Chief of Detectives John Hoffman and removed Inspector Raymond Boettcher of the Bethune Station from active duty. The old district police inspector system was then abolished by Eaman. This move brought more resignations.

On January 15, 1940, the motion for a Robinson mistrial was denied, as was a motion for a directed verdict of acquittal by defense attorneys in the Robinson case. That same day, the defense called Irving Feldman to the witness stand. Feldman told the court that he operated several bookmaking joints in the city. According to Feldman, Dr. Robinson had placed a bet on a horse race the day before the holdup. Robinson lost $3,440 on the race. Feldman and the three other defendants had gone to Dr. Robinson's office on July 8 to collect the money. Dr. Robinson only had $2,600 of the total owed to Feldman. He gave the men this money and the five guns found in the car as collateral on the balance of the debt. Robinson then suggested that the men stage a phony holdup so that he could collect the money he lost on the race through his holdup insurance and pay off the balance of the gambling debt. Feldman testified that Robinson had cut the telephone wires with a scissors and told him and Jacobs to bind him with adhesive tape to make the holdup look good to his wife and secretary. "Both women came in just as we were leaving with the money and the pistols," said Feldman. "I told Mrs. Wolfe [Florence Wolfe, the doctor's secretary] that the doctor was in the other office and to be quiet, and he would take care of everything." Feldman then explained to the court that when he and Jacobs left the building, they met Cooper and Holtzman on Custer Avenue. In order to escape the heavy traffic on Woodward during lunch hour, the men drove down an alley where they were unexpectedly stopped and arrested by Inspector Myers.

Farrish and Brouillet were picked up later the same week by State Police in Erie, Pennsylvania. Warrants had been issued for their arrest. The two detectives were rushed back to Detroit Recorders Court, where they were brought before Judge Thomas Cotter. They had been out of the state for five days. Cotter found both men in contempt of court and sentenced them to five days in jail. Brouillet admitted that he had lied on the witness stand earlier, when he had stated that Inspector Myers ordered him and Farrish to give some of the evidence money back to Dr. Robinson. Farrish gave Robinson $1,000, and Robinson in appreciation had given each detective $75 for their services. Brouillet confessed that he then changed the property sheet from $1,600 to $600. Both detectives, Farrish and Brouillet, admitted that Inspector Raymond Boettcher of the Bethune Station and other high-ranking officers at police headquarters knew of the coverup for months. Two days after the holdup, Dr. Robinson called and complained to Farrish and Brouillet that it cost him several hundred dollars more in bribes to get out of the station.

On January 17, 1940, the Robinson case was given to the jury. It was up to the people to decide if Dr. Robinson had been the victim of a holdup on July 8, 1939, or merely paying off a gambling debt.

Defense attorney Sidney Sherman made the argument in his closing statement before the jury that if this had been a real holdup, Holtzman would have never stopped the car for Inspector Myers. "If they were the desperate men they are depicted and were fleeing a holdup, they would have knocked Myers aside with the fender of their car or blown the top of his head off with the pistols," Sherman contended. The jury was out two hours and 40 minutes and brought in a verdict of acquittal for the Purple Gang defendants. The four men were immediately taken into police custody after the verdict was read. A warrant had been issued on orders from Judge Ferguson. The new charge was carrying concealed weapons.

Detectives Farrish and Brouillet were taken before the grand jury. In testimony, the former officers described how Joe Holtzman told them that $1,000 was paid to Inspector Boettcher to let Dr. Robinson get back some of the confiscated holdup money that was to be used as evidence. Farrish and Brouillet also admitted that Robinson gave them $75 each in gratitude for giving him back $1,000 of the holdup money. The detectives told Judge Ferguson that several days after the holdup, they ran into Sammy Millman and Scotty Silverstein. Millman and Silverstein offered the detectives $1,000 to try and fix the case by getting the armed-robbery charges dropped. Farrish and Brouillet stated that they took $300 and were promised the other $700 if they could get the case dismissed. During this same period, both men admitted attending a conference at an attorney's house. Present at this meeting were Sam Millman, Scotty Silverstein, and an official from the Wayne County Prosecutor's

Office. The purpose of the gathering was to discuss how they might get the case thrown out or if necessary, get the charges reduced to carrying concealed weapons.

At their examination, all four Purple Gangsters acquitted in the Robinson holdup trial pleaded not guilty to the new charge of carrying concealed weapons. They were promptly ordered to appear before Judge Ferguson on charges growing out of Farrish and Brouillet's confessions. All four defendants were charged with conspiracy to obstruct justice.

On January 19, 1940, acting on warrants issued by Judge Ferguson, police arrested Purple Gang defense attorney Sidney Sherman and former Purple Sam Millman. Both men were officially charged with conspiracy to obstruct justice in the Robinson case. Four more men were also being sought on the same charges. The list included former Purple Gangsters Izzy Bernstein and Jacob "Scotty" Silverstein, Dr. Martin Robinson, and Assistant Wayne County Prosecutor Robert Perretto. Judge Ferguson had received information that Perretto was involved in the conspiracy and was given the responsibility of trying to fix the case in the prosecutor's office. Perretto had been suspended from his position in the prosecutor's office several days earlier.

Detailed in the grand jury warrant against the six suspects for conspiracy to obstruct justice were the specifics of the case. On July 10, 1939, Holtzman, Cooper, Jacobs, and Feldman had been jailed on charges of armed robbery. That same day Farrish, Brouillet, and the other defendants had met at the home of attorney Sidney Sherman. According to the grand jury testimony of Farrish and Brouillet, plans were made at this meeting to get the armed-robbery case quashed or reduced to a charge of carrying concealed weapons. If the case was reduced to the weapons charge, Holtzman was to take the responsibility for the guns. The reason for this was that Holtzman was the only one of the holdup suspects that did not have a police record. At that time, it was agreed that Dr. Robinson would fail to identify the four men as the bandits who had robbed him. Later, the conspirators offered Detectives Farrish and Brouillet $1,000 to fix the case. Robert Perretto, the Assistant Wayne County Prosecutor in charge of the holdup case, agreed to try to get the charges reduced, and he made suggestions at the meeting of how this could be accomplished.

As a result of these revelations before the Ferguson Grand Jury, all six of these men and the four Robinson case defendants were officially charged with conspiracy to obstruct justice. Sherman and Millman were arrested on January 19, 1940. The attorney was arrested in his downtown Detroit law office, located in the Barlum Tower. When Sherman was registered and fingerprinted at Detroit police headquarters, he appeared to be on the verge of a breakdown. With tears streaming down his face, he said, "There is nothing to this! I have never been arrested before, not even for a traffic ticket. This is all wrong!"

By January 21, 1940, Superintendent of Police Fred Frahm had been fired, Chief of Detectives John Hoffman had resigned. Raymond Boettcher, Uniform Division Inspector at Bethune Station, was suspended and appeared before the Ferguson Grand Jury. The district police inspector system was abolished by Commissioner Eaman, and four of five district inspectors had resigned. These men included self-proclaimed Purple Gang nemesis Henry J. Garvin. The Detroit Police Department was in turmoil.

On March 15, 1940, Feldman, Holtzman, Jacobs, and Cooper were convicted of carrying concealed weapons in Detroit Recorders Court. Feldman, Jacobs, and Cooper were sentenced to serve 2½ to 5 years in state prison. Holtzman was given 5 years' probation. On May 21, 1940, the warrant against Sidney Sherman was officially dropped on a motion from his attorney. Assistant Prosecutor Robert Perretto was eventually reinstated, and the conspiracy charge against him was dropped on May 24, 1940. Charges against both Perretto and Sherman were unsubstantiated and vague. Sherman continued to practice criminal law for many years afterwards, but close friends maintain that he was never the same after having been accused of the Ferguson charges. On May 27, 1940, Dr. Martin Robinson and Sam Millman were found guilty of conspiracy to obstruct justice. On November 13, 1940, Robinson was sentenced to 3 to 5 years in state prison. Millman received a sentence of 2 to 5 years.

The grand jury testimony of Detectives Farrish and Brouillet implicated Inspector Raymond Boettcher in the Robinson case. It was Boettcher's testimony that really blew the lid off the police department graft investigation. Shortly after Inspector Boettcher was called before the Ferguson Grand Jury in the middle of January 1940, he decided to become a state's witness and was granted immunity in the case. Boettcher's testimony created a sensation in Detroit. The inspector told the grand jury that he had been the "bag man" (payoff man) for the $50 million a year numbers rackets in

Detroit. Boettcher described himself as the payoff man at Detroit police headquarters and City Hall. He received money every month from Elmer "Buff" Ryan. Ryan, a former gambler, was the gambling syndicate's contact man with Detroit police headquarters. The monthly payments were for protection from the Detroit Police Department and City Hall. Boettcher told the grand jury an amazing story. He described in detail how he personally paid former Mayor Richard Reading and his son, Richard Jr., more than $4,000 a month in graft. Boettcher stated that he served in the capacity of payoff man between the gamblers and city officials for 33 months. "Thanksgiving came every month in the City Hall and police department," Boettcher told the grand jury. Inspectors' jobs in the police department could be purchased for $1,500 each. Other positions could also be secured for the right cash payments. Boettcher testified that he paid monthly graft allowances to Superintendent of Police Fred Frahm and many other high-ranking police officials. The former inspector explained how he paid Frahm between $1,000 and $1,800 every month. Boettcher would often hand Frahm the money in a men's room at Detroit police headquarters. "Slip it to me, kid," the superintendent would say to Boettcher, as he handed Frahm the graft payment. The inspector called the Robinson case a jinx. Boettcher told the grand jury that when the $1,000 in recovered robbery loot was returned to Robinson the day of the holdup, Robinson had paid him and another officer $200 apiece in appreciation. Boettcher had been present at the Bethune Station the day Inspector Myers walked in with the four reputed bandits and the holdup money. The inspector had made the mistake of being photographed counting the holdup money by a press photographer. Boettcher believed that this photograph was what tied him to the Robinson case. When questioned by Special Prosecutor O'Hara, Boettcher replied, "I never counted any of the money, at no time did I handle the money. The only thing I got was a $200 gift from Robinson." "I should have thrown Robinson out the window when he offered me $200. I sincerely wish I had," Boettcher lamented.

It seemed as though the majority of officials in the police department and City Hall were on Buff Ryan's payroll. It was later discovered that Wayne County Prosecutor Duncan C. McCrea was one of the worst "grifters" (police slang for anyone who takes graft). At first, McCrea demanded $1,500 a month from the handbook operators. Later, the price for protection from the prosecutor's office was raised to $3,000 a month. Still not satisfied with this figure, McCrea sent a messenger around to every handbook in the city with address forms. The forms were returned to McCrea, who then levied a $5 a week tax on every handbook in Detroit through Consolidated News Service. With more than 700 handbooks in the city, this amounted to a princely sum.

Boettcher was shocked when he learned that even the Wayne County Prosecutor was on "Buff" Ryan's payroll. The former Inspector had never known anything about that angle of the gambling syndicate's graft payments. Both Wayne County Prosecutor Duncan C. McCrea and Wayne County Sheriff Thomas Wilcox were removed from office and later convicted of taking graft for offering protection. Both men were sentenced to serve $4^{1}/_{2}$ to 5 years in state prison.

Aside from city officials and police department brass, hundreds of bookmakers, numbers operators, and organized crime figures associated with the Detroit gambling industry were brought before Judge Ferguson. In August of 1940, both Abe and Joe Bernstein were called before the grand jury to explain their interests in the Consolidated News Service. Consolidated provided horse-race information to all of the Detroit area handbooks. According to testimony from various gamblers, the Purple Gang had muscled their way into the Consolidated News Service in 1929. This was accomplished by kidnapping one of the principal owners and holding him for ransom. Some gamblers thought the Purples had been given 25 percent of Consolidated. Others thought it was much more. Testimony also showed that the Consolidated News Service paid William C. Rick, Commander of Central Station, $100 a month. The news service also paid the Wayne County Prosecutor's Office $1,500 a month in 1934 and 1935. In 1935, Consolidated was taken over by the Nationwide News Service of Chicago. At that time the Purples were no longer the dominant power in the Detroit underworld. Abe and Joe Bernstein were out.

In November of 1943, Isadore Bernstein was finally arrested in Los Angeles. He was later extradited back to Detroit to stand trial on the conspiracy to obstruct justice charges growing out of the Robinson case. Bernstein described himself as a retired Detroit businessman, now residing in Beverly Hills, California. On December 17, 1943, he walked into Detroit police headquarters with Lt. Marvin Lane, the officer that had taken him back to Michigan. "Hello, Izzy," said Inspector Edward

Graff. "My name is Irving," said Bernstein with dignity, "and this is another bum rap." Bernstein was arraigned and released on bail. Almost three years later, Bernstein appeared with his lawyer in Detroit Recorders Court shortly before his case was to go to trial. Bernstein pleaded guilty. The judge accepted the plea, fined him $2,500 plus $250 court costs, and he was released.

On October 15, 1946, the last defendant untried on charges growing out of the Robinson case stood before Judge Arthur E. Gordon in Recorders Court. Found guilty of conspiracy to obstruct justice, Jacob "Scotty" Silverstein was fined $1,000 plus $250 court costs. Silverstein's previous court dates had been waived because he was serving with the U.S. Army in Italy. Silverstein was seriously wounded overseas and returned to the U.S. eight months earlier. No doubt his military record figured into his light sentence. Elmer "Buff" Ryan was later convicted in a policy and numbers case and sentenced to 1-5 years. Judge Homer Ferguson went on to become a U.S. senator, and Chester O'Hara a Wayne County circuit judge.

• • •

In the final analysis, most of the officials who professed shock by the original charges were hit with indictments. In the end, Mayor Richard Reading, his son Richard Jr., many top police officers and lesser policemen, Wayne County Sheriff Thomas Wilcox, and Prosecutor Duncan McCrea were all convicted, removed from their posts, and served prison time. In all, the Ferguson Grand Jury indicted 360 persons, including 75 public officials and 81 racketeers. More than 150 went to prison over a four-year period. Chances are that all of it would have been overlooked had it not been for the dramatic suicide/murder of Janet MacDonald, which made the corruption impossible for even corrupt officials to overlook.

After a short time, the handbook and numbers rackets once again appeared in Detroit. The Ferguson Grand Jury investigation, however, practically ended the old-time roadhouse and casino-style gambling that had run wide open in Wayne and Macomb Counties for years. The investigation did not stop official corruption, but was a wake-up call to the community and to public and law-enforcement officials.

# Dangerous Freelancers

"You'd better pick up Eddie Sarkesian if you don't want to find him full of lead. He's on the spot. He's been shaking down bookies. The boys are after him. He's got a gun!"
—*Anonymous phone call tip to Detroit police, August 16, 1944*

"I've got heavy business, someone important to meet. I don't think I'll ever be back. If I don't show up, the station is yours."
—*Last known words of Detroit mobster Chris Scroy, April 8, 1959*

The Ferguson Grand Jury investigation essentially destroyed the old-style roadhouse gambling operations in the Detroit area. Many Prohibition era gamblers left the state. Some went to Hallendale, Florida, where their gambling expertise was in demand. These men were sought out by the New York and Chicago Mobs and offered good jobs in the Florida casino business and later in Las Vegas.

The Italian Mob was in firm control of the Detroit underworld by the early '40s. They were heavily involved in bookmaking and numbers in Detroit. Both of these types of operations could be easily concealed. Operators who were not directly connected to the Detroit Mafia organization paid a street tax to the Mob to remain in business. However, there were always rebel underworld operators in Detroit who tried to buck the system. Some of these men were former Prohibition era gangsters who had thrived during the period when the Purple Gang ceased to exist in the mid-'30s, and the Italian Mob took over. Often they were thugs who had either worked for the Purples or the local Mafia family and decided they wanted a piece of the action for themselves.

• • •

### EDDIE SARKESIAN

At approximately 11 p.m. on August 16, 1944, residents in a neighborhood near the east side of Detroit were startled by the sound of gunfire. Witnesses later told police that they heard seven or eight shots and saw a Cadillac convertible run up over the curb close to a busy nearby intersection and come to a stop. Three men were seen running from the car. When police arrived, they found a man slumped over the steering wheel. Although he had been shot in the head at close range and was unconscious, he was still alive. Detroit homicide detectives quickly identified the gravely wounded man as Eddie Sarkesian, a freelance thug and stick-up man who often worked as a collector for the Detroit Mob. He died en route to the hospital. It was later discovered that he had been shot six times in the head by someone who had been sitting next to him in the front seat of the car.

Earlier that day, someone had called Detroit police headquarters and stated that the Mob was hunting Sarkesian and if they did not act, he would be murdered. Detectives were looking for Sarkesian when they received word that he had been shot. Crime scene investigators assumed that Eddie Sarkesian was riding with men he trusted. A man seated in the back seat had evidently grabbed Sarkesian around the neck while he was driving and held him as he was shot. Detectives surmised that a moment before he was shot Sarkesian realized that his friends were in reality his executioners. He had pulled his revolver, which was knocked out of his hand when his assassin struck him with the barrel of the pistol that he used to dispatch Sarkesian a moment later. Except for a bruise on his right hand, there were no other signs of a struggle. Eddie's gun lay in a pool of blood on the floor of the car, fully loaded. His murder was a long time in coming.

Eddie Sarkesian's life had been a long, hard-luck story. Born in East St. Louis, Illinois, in 1914, Sarkesian's parents were both Middle Eastern immigrants. The family moved to Detroit in 1919, where Eddie essentially grew up on the street. As a teenager, he got involved in amateur boxing and became a heavyweight fighter of indifferent ability. His training, however, gave him a definite edge on the street.

By the late '20s, Eddie was regularly getting into trouble with the law. From petty theft and breaking and entering he quickly graduated into strong-arm work. Sarkesian was 5'8" and 180 pounds and was tough. He had a reputation in the Detroit underworld of being totally unprincipled and ruthless. While still in his late teens, local mobsters often used Sarkesian's strong-arm talents for collecting bookie debts and loan shark money. By the early

'30s, Sarkesian grew impatient with his progress in the Detroit underworld. Eddie and a partner began sticking up Detroit area beer gardens. In June of 1934 Sarkesian got into a scuffle with a Detroit beer-joint owner during a holdup and shot the man in the leg. He was quickly arrested and convicted in Detroit Recorders Court of armed robbery. On September 11, 1934, Sarkesian was sentenced to serve from 10 to 30 years in Marquette Prison. Eddie was just 20 years old at the time of his sentence.

Sarkesian served eight years in prison and was paroled in 1942 on the condition that he enlist in the army. He quickly enlisted but was discharged for medical reasons after serving only a few months. Once he was back on the street, Sarkesian began to realize that things had changed considerably in the Detroit underworld since he had gone to prison. He kept in shape while he was incarcerated and even worked for a short time as a professional fighter after he was discharged. Lacking ability as a full-time pugilist, Eddie put his physical skills to work as a bouncer in a Hamtramck bowling alley and lounge. Sarkesian was not happy with the money he was making and went back to work once again as a collector for the Detroit Mob. He made the rounds of bookie joints and underworld hangouts, where he was known and feared as a Mob muscleman. Sarkesian's strong-arm ability was respected by the Detroit Mob, but Eddie again grew tired of the work and longed for a bigger piece of the action. This was an impossibility in the Detroit underworld of the '40s. The local Mafia had most of the lucrative rackets locked up. Nobody operated in the wartime Detroit underworld without the okay from the local

Mafia bosses.

Sometime in 1943 Sarkesian and a former Purple Gangster named Harry "Chink" Meltzer decided to go into business sticking up bookmakers who were operating under the protection of the Mob. The pair believed that their plan was foolproof. Meltzer, a former bookmaker himself, personally knew many of the Detroit area gambling operators. He would visit various bookmaking establishments and make a note of when the daily bet money was transferred from the bookmaker to a local bank. A messenger would usually carry the money to the bank. Meltzer served as the "finger man" by pointing out the messenger to Eddie Sarkesian, who would be waiting nearby. Sarkesian would put a gun against the back of the messenger's head and relieve him of his deposit money. The proceeds were then divided between Sarkesian and Meltzer. The bookmakers couldn't go to the police but soon began complaining bitterly to their Mafia protectors about their losses. For a while, this system worked efficiently. Meltzer and Sarkesian continued to rob Detroit and Hamtramck bookmakers. Like many high-profile gangsters before him, either Sarkesian believed that the Mob was afraid to interfere or he had a suicidal death wish.

Sarkesian soon branched out into hijacking liquor trucks and then selling the stolen liquor to bars in Detroit and surrounding communities. For more than a year, Sarkesian continued to shake down Detroit area bookmakers with his various partners. Finally, he was approached by chief Detroit Mob enforcer Mike Rubino and warned to lay off the handbook robberies. Sarkesian agreed but continued robbing handbooks. It was assumed by Detroit police that his actions led to his murder on August 16, 1944.

But there was another theory floating around the Detroit underworld. It was believed that Sarkesian had been given $7,500 by some former Purple Gangsters in order to pay off some jockeys and fix several races at the Detroit Race Track. Sarkesian, according to this account, made off with the money, and a Purple Gang associate put up $5,000 to have Sarkesian killed.

Shortly after the murder, Eddie's 20-year-old wife Mary was questioned about his business and his associates. The couple had only been married two weeks when Sarkesian was murdered. She told detectives that she didn't know how her husband made his living. The only evidence police discovered was a .32 caliber pistol found by two boys the day after Sarkesian was murdered. Ballistics tests proved that this was the weapon used to murder Sarkesian. His murder was a warning sent to free-lance underworld operators, letting them know that they were not welcome in Detroit. It would be a losing proposition for anyone to rebel against local Mob authority.

• • •

## The Scroy Brothers

On the afternoon of June 12, 1948, Sam Scroy and his cousin, Pete Lucido, left their homes for a meeting in downtown Detroit with mobster Maxie Stern. Scroy and Lucido were professional gamblers and bookmakers. Stern was a lieutenant of Detroit Mob boss Pete Licavoli and was one of the Italian Mob's gambling czars in the Detroit and Windsor, Ontario, area. The purpose of the meeting was reportedly to get permission for the Scroy brothers and Lucido to set up a handbook in Windsor. Sam Scroy and Pete Lucido were never seen again. The next day the families of the two men reported them missing. Detroit police later found Sam Scroy's car parked in a downtown Detroit lot. Several days later Lucido's car was discovered by detectives near Toledo, Ohio. Police found the trunk on Lucido's car open. When they looked inside, all they found were two maroon buttons. There was no evidence of foul play. Members of the Lucido family later identified the buttons as being off the shirt that Lucido wore the day he disappeared.

Detroit police talked to an employee of Sam Scroy's named Tony Marino. Marino worked in one of the Scroy brothers' Detroit handbooks. He claimed he had a brief conversation with the two men the day they disappeared. Nothing seemed out of the ordinary at that time. Underworld informants told detectives that the two men had been murdered by the Detroit Mob for trying to break into the Windsor gambling rackets the year before. The two men were reported to be partners in a Detroit book-making business and were in financial difficulty over recent gambling losses. Detroit mobsters Anthony (Tony Jack) Giacalone, Joe "Scarface" Bommarito, Dave Feldman, and Max Stern, known associates of Scroy and Lucido, were picked up for questioning and released. For almost two years, the disappearance of the two men remained a mystery.

On the evening of February 17, 1950, Chris Scroy, Sam's older brother, pulled his car up to the curb near Moses Joseph's coffee house in Detroit. Chris was a tough, independent bookmaker and local racketeer who once had close connections to the Detroit Mafia family. These contacts had soured since the disappearance of his younger brother, Sam.

As Chris Scroy sat in his car and waited patiently in the dusk of that frigid February evening, he soon saw a familiar car pull up. Pulling a Mauser pistol out of his overcoat and checking the clip, he quickly stepped out of his vehicle and walked up to where the driver was backing the car into a parking space. Without saying a word, Chris Scroy emptied the clip into the car. The force of the blasts threw the driver back against his seat, and he slumped down to the floor. Chris Scroy had just shot Maxie Stern. Thinking Stern was dead, Scroy turned, walked back to his car, and drove away.

A friend of Stern's who had been waiting for Maxie in the coffee shop rushed him to the hospital. Police quickly arrived at the scene of the shooting. Nine shots had penetrated Stern's car. Only two hit Stern. Although he was listed in critical condition, doctors had confidence he would live. At the time of his attempted murder, Max Stern was 37 years old. He was known in the Detroit underworld as an enforcer and as the chief of local gambling operations for the Italian Mob.

Chris Scroy drove to Belle Isle, a city park in the Detroit River. As he drove over the Belle Isle Bridge, he pitched the Mauser pistol that he used to shoot Stern into the river. The next day he was arrested by Detroit police and charged with assault with intent to commit murder. Scroy had been recognized by people inside the coffee shop the night he shot Stern. Scroy denied the charge and was released. On March 9, 1950, Scroy was arrested at his home. He was taken to Detroit police headquarters and made a full confession. Scroy told police that he held

Stern responsible for the murder of his younger brother, Sam, and his cousin, Pete Lucido. That was why he had shot Stern.

Of the incident Scroy confessed, "The night of the shooting I went to Congress Street in Detroit next to Moses Joseph's coffee house because I knew Stern came there. When he pulled up in his car, I walked up and started shooting. After my gun was empty, I walked around the corner, got in my car, and took off."

Chris Scroy also blamed Mob boss Pete Licavoli and Joe "Scarface" Bommarito for his brother's murder. Scroy told homicide detectives that he had really wanted to kill Licavoli or Bommarito. "They run the Sicilian clique that is taking over everything," Scroy told police. For four consecutive weeks, Chris Scroy had hidden in bushes near Joe Bommarito's Detroit home hoping to ambush the Mafia capo, but Bommarito never appeared.

"Stern works for them," Scroy told police. "They are heads of the Detroit syndicate." When Scroy was told that Stern had only been shot twice, he was surprised. "He must have been wearing a bulletproof vest," Scroy explained. "I'm not that bad of a shot. Every time I fired a round, he squirmed."

There had been bad blood between the Scroy brothers and Max Stern for more than 10 years. According to Chris Scroy, the trouble began in 1940. Stern's brother-in-law, Ben Griesman, had tried to shortchange Chris Scroy on the sale of some horse-racing tip sheets. The quick-tempered Scroy slapped Griesman, who complained about the incident to Stern. The next day, according to Scroy, Stern came around with a gun and forced Scroy and his younger brother to get into his car. As they were driving out of the city, Stern spotted a police car and was momentarily distracted. At that point, according to Chris Scroy, he had knocked the pistol out of Stern's hand, and he and his brother jumped out of the car. Several days later, Chris and Sam Scroy ran into Max Stern in a downtown Detroit nightclub. Sam Scroy wanted to shoot Stern on the spot, but Chris claimed he had talked him out of it. Instead, Sam Scroy walked up to Stern and warned him to stop throwing his weight around on Woodward Avenue.

Chris Scroy told Detroit police that he, Sam, and their cousin, Pete Lucido, had operated a Detroit bookmaking business independently of the Detroit Mob. At that time, they also owned a news stand in downtown Detroit near the Detroit/Windsor tunnel. In 1947, they attempted to start a horse-betting operation in Windsor. In order to solicit customers, they would approach people waiting at the tunnel bus stop for the Windsor bus. Scroy stated that the Licavoli faction of the Detroit Mob controlled all gambling in Windsor. By agreement with the local police, Scroy's Windsor competitors would close. The Scroy brothers' Windsor handbook would then be raided and busted up. Continued harassment by Windsor law-enforcement friendly to the Licavoli combine finally forced the Scroy brothers out of business in Windsor. Chris and Sam then sold the handbook to their cousin, Pete Lucido. "Then that Sicilian bunch muscled in and took over Windsor," Scroy told police. "They had the wire service, they just ran things. I'm a Sicilian myself but not one of their kind," Chris Scroy explained. "I never had a gun and never hurt anybody until my brother disappeared."

According to Chris Scroy, Sam and Pete Lucido

were murdered because Pete Licavoli and others associated with the Windsor race wire service believed that the Scroy brothers and Lucido were trying to muscle in on their gambling territory. Licavoli and other Detroit Mob figures had actually had a meeting with the Scroy brothers and Lucido and offered to pay them $45 a week to stay out of Windsor.

Another rumor that circulated in the Detroit underworld at that time was that the Scroy brothers were receiving race wire information from Howard Kerr, a former Chicago bookmaker and big-time gambling operator in Windsor. Kerr was reported to be operating with the okay from Detroit Mob boss Pete Corrado. When the Detroit Mob wanted the Scroy brothers out of Windsor, Kerr had given Lucido $7,500 to close his operation and stay out of gambling in the Windsor area. Prior to the disappearance of Sam Scroy and Pete Lucido, there had been numerous raids by Windsor police who were not on the payroll of the Detroit Mob. These raids were on the Polo Club operated by Kerr and on numerous other Detroit Mob operations in Windsor. Pete Lucido was believed responsible for tipping off the police. On June 12, 1948, the Windsor police raided and busted up the race wire headquarters of the Detroit Mob. That night Sam Scroy and Pete Lucido were called to a meeting and disappeared.

The trial of Chris Scroy for assault with intent to commit murder opened in Detroit Recorders Court on June 14, 1950. In typical underworld fashion, Max Stern denied that Scroy had shot him. "Scroy and I have been friends since we sold papers together as kids," Stern told the court. The jury wasn't convinced. On June 20, 1950, Chris Scroy was convicted of the felony charge. Two weeks later, Scroy was sentenced to serve 7 to 30 years in Jackson Prison. Scroy was 40 years old. Shortly after Chris Scroy was convicted, Detroit police received information that Sam Scroy and Lucido had been murdered by the Detroit Mob, and their bodies had been disposed of in a rock quarry somewhere between Detroit and Toledo.

While Chris Scroy was serving his sentence, Detroit police received other information from underworld sources about the murders of Sam Scroy and Pete Lucido. According to this story, Lucido and Scroy, who were known by police as sometime labor racketeers, had been paid $2,000 cash by a local Mob boss to beat two members of the Briggs UAW-CIO local. The purpose of this strong-arm work was to help certain anti-Reuther forces within the UAW gain control of the local. The Mob saw this as a chance to form an alliance with the anti-Reuther forces in the auto workers union and to profit enormously by this partnership. Scroy and Lucido did a good job and were given another strong-arm assignment. This time Scroy and Lucido decided to give the job to other muscle men for $400. The Detroit Mob found out about the subcontracting deal and only paid the two racketeers $400 when the assignment was completed. Scroy and Lucido were rankled by this gesture. On April 20, 1948, Walter Reuther was shot through the kitchen window of his home. Supposedly, Sam Scroy and Lucido knew specifics about the Detroit Mob's involvement with the Reuther shooting and threatened to go to the police. As a result, they were killed.

Chris Scroy was released from Jackson Prison on July 14, 1955. He later opened a gas station in St.

Clair Shores, a Detroit suburb. It was eventually discovered that the gas station was a front for a new handbook operation. On the afternoon of April 10, 1959, Scroy left the station telling an employee that he had an urgent meeting. The next day he was reported missing by his family. For 18 months his disappearance remained a mystery. On October 20, 1960, the dismembered body of Chris Scroy was discovered in seven burlap sacks in a ditch near Mt. Clemens, Michigan. State Police and St. Clair Shores police were notified of the grisly discovery. The body was later positively identified by fingerprints and clothing found with the remains. Dr. Richard Olsen, a Pontiac, Michigan, pathologist, conducted the post-mortem exam. According to Olsen's report, Scroy had been killed by several hard blows to the head and had been dead approximately 18 months. The body was covered with lime and then buried. For some reason, several weeks before Scroy's remains were discovered, someone had dug up the body, dismembered it, and dumped it in a north Macomb County field. Police theorized that when the killers checked the body and found it still fairly well intact, they chopped it up and left it exhumed, possibly as another warning not to do business in their town.

• • •

By the late '40s, the Detroit Mafia family had established themselves as the absolute rulers of the Detroit underworld. Eddie Sarkesian and the Scroy brothers were among the last of the Prohibition era rebels. For more than 40 years, the Detroit Mob was able to maintain a low profile while reaping fantastic profits in legitimate businesses and the rackets. Only the advent of a federal law-enforcement assault on the Detroit Mob in the 1990s using the RICO law (Racketeer Influenced and Corrupt Organizations) and aging leadership of the Detroit Mob marked the beginning of the end for the old-style organization.

# Bibliography

**Books**

Abadansky, Howard. *Organized Crime*. Chicago: Nelson-Hall Publishers, 1997.

Albini, Joseph L. *The American Mafia: Genesis of a Legend*. New York: Appleton-Century-Crofts, 1971.

Alix, Ernest Kahlar. *Ransom Kidnapping in America 1874-1975: The Creation of a Capital Crime*. Carbondale, IL: Southern Illinois University Press, 1978.

Allen, Edward J. *Merchants of Menace: The Mafia*. Springfield, IL: Charles C. Thomas Publishers, 1962.

Asher, Cash. *Sacred Cows: A Story of the Recall of Mayor Bowles*. Detroit: Published by the author, 1931.

Behr, Edward. *Prohibition: Thirteen Years That Changed America*. New York: Arcade Publishing, 1996.

Bonnano, Bill. *Bound by Honor: A Mafioso's Story*. New York: St. Martin's Press, 1998.

Bruns, Roger A. *The Bandit Kings*. New York: Crown Publishers, 1995.

Cashman, Sean Dennis. *Prohibition: The Lie of the Land*. New York: The Free Press, 1981.

Catanzano, Raimondo. *Men of Respect: A Social History of the Sicilian Mafia*. New York: The Free Press, 1992.

Coffee, Thomas M. *The Long Thirst: Prohibition in America 1920-1933*. New York: W.W. Norton & Company, 1975.

Cressey, Donald R. *Theft of the Nation: The Structure and Operations of Organized Crime in America*. New York:

Harper and Row Publishers, 1969.

Einstein, Izzy. *Prohibition Agent No. 1*. New York: Frederick Stokes and Co., 1932.

Engelman, Larry. *Intemperance: The Lost War Against Liquor*. New York: The Free Press, 1979.

Gervais, G.H. *The Rumrunners: A Prohibition Era Scrapbook*. Scarborough, Ontario: Firefly Books Ltd., 1980.

Gray, James H. *The Roar of the Twenties*. Ontario: MacMillan of Canada, 1975.

Helmer, William J. *The Gun That Made the Twenties Roar*. Toronto, Ontario: The MacMillan Co., 1969.

Helmer, William, with Steve Mattix. *Public Enemies: America's Criminal Past 1919-1940*. New York: Checkmark Books, 1998.

Hess, Henner. *Mafia and Mafioso*. New York: New York University Press, 1998.

Hoover, J. Edgar. *Persons in Hiding*. New York: Little Brown Co., 1938.

Hopkins, Ernest Jerome. *Our Lawless Police*. New York: Viking Press, 1931.

Hunt, C.W. *Booze, Boats and Billions: Smuggling Liquid Gold*. Ontario: McClelland and Stewart, 1988.

Illman, Harry R. *Unholy Toledo*. San Francisco: Polemic Press Publications, 1985.

Kavieff, Paul R. *The Purple Gang: Organized Crime in Detroit 1910-1945*. New York: Barricade Books, 2000.

Kelly, Robert J. *Encyclopedia of Organized Crime in the United States: From Capone to the New Urban Underworld*. Westport, CT: Greenwood Press, 2000.

Kirkpatrick. E.E. *Crimes' Paradise*. San Antonio, TX: The Naylor Company, 1934.

Kobler, John. *Ardent Spirits: The Rise and Fall of Prohibition*. New York: G.P. Putnam's Sons, 1970.

Lee, Henry. *How Dry We Were: Prohibition Revisited*. Englewood Cliffs, NJ: Prentice Hall, 1975.

Lynch, Dennis Tilden. *Criminals and Politicians*. New York: The MacMillan Co., 1932.

Mason, Philip P. *Rumrunning and the Roaring Twenties: Prohibition on the Michigan-Ontario Waterway*. Detroit: Wayne State University Press, 1995.

Merz, Charles. *The Dry Decade*. New York: Doubleday, Doran Publishers, 1931.

Nelli, Humbert S. *The Business of Crime: Italians and Syndicate Crime in the United States.* New York: Oxford University Press, 1976.

Partridge, Eric. *A Dictionary of the Underworld.* New York: The MacMillan Co., 1950.

Perello, Rick. *To Kill the Irishman: The War That Crippled the Mafia.* Cleveland: Next Hat Press, 1998.

Pitkin, Thomas Monroe, and Cordasco Francesco. *The Black Hand: A Chapter in Ethnic Crime.* Tutowa, NJ: Rowman and Littlefield, 1977.

Purvis, Melvin. *American Agent.* New York: Doubleday, Doran & Co., 1936.

Reed, Lear B. *Human Wolves.* Kansas City: Brown White-Lowell Press, 1941.

Reid, Ed. *The Grim Reapers: The Anatomy of Organized Crime in America.* Chicago: Henry Regnery Co., 1969.

Rudell, Mary E. (Ed.) *Detroit Murders.* New York: Duell, Sloan and Pearce, 1948.

Ruth, David E. *Inventing the Public Enemy: The Gangster in American Culture 1918-1934.* Chicago: The University of Chicago Press, 1996.

Scott, George Ryley. *The History of Capital Punishment.* London: Torchstream Publishers, 1950.

Seruadio, Gaia. *Mafioso: A History of the Mafia from its Origins to the Present.* New York: Stein and Day, 1976.

Sheridan, Leo W. *I Killed for the Law.* New York: Stackpole Sons, 1938.

Sullivan, Edward Dean. *The Snatch Racket.* New York: The Vanguard Press, 1932.

Woodford, Frank B. *Alex J. Groesbeck: Portrait of a Public Man.* Detroit: Wayne State University Press, 1962.

Woodford, Frank B., and Arthur M. Woodford. *All Our Yesterdays: A Brief History of Detroit.* Detroit: Wayne State University Press, 1969.

## Michigan State Police Criminal Complaints

Case No. 2206; Location: St. Joseph, Michigan, Berrien County; Crime: Murder; Date: December 14, 1929; Victim: Charles L. Skelly; Suspect: Fred Burke alias Dane.

Case No. 2389: County: Wayne; Officers: William Watkins;

Location: Detroit; Date: July 1, 1925; Crime: Bank Robbery; Victim: People's Wayne County Bank; Suspect: Frank Cammarata.

Case No. 1136; Location: Cassopolis; Crime: Bank Robbery; Date: November 24, 1926; Victim: First National Bank; Suspects: Chester Tutha, Joe Konen, James Allen, Sam Bokosky, Clarence Madden, and Steven Racskewski.

Case No. 5970; Location: Albion, Calhoun County, Michigan; Crime: B&E Store and Safe Robbery; Date: March 9, 1936; Victim: Kroger Store; Suspects: Louis Fleisher, Chester Tutha, Sam Bernstein, Harry Fleisher.

Case No. 5954; Location: Jackson, Michigan, Jackson County; Crime: B&E and Safe Robbery; Date: May 11, 1936; Victim: Isabel Seed Co.; Suspects: Louis Fleisher, Sam Bernstein, Chester Tutha, John Godlewski, Robert Deptla.

Case No. 5954; Location: Jackson, Michigan, Jackson County, Crime: B&E and Safe Robbery; Date: June 2, 1936; Victim: Riverside Packing Co.; Suspects: Louis Fleisher, Sam Bernstein, Chester Tutha, John Godlewski, Robert Deptla.

**Newspapers**
*Detroit Evening Times*
*Detroit Free Press*
*Detroit News*
*Hamtramck Citizen*
*Pontiac Press*

# Index

# Acknowledgments

Many people helped me in assembling research material used in *The Violent Years*. I would like to thank Pat Zacharias and her staff at the *Detroit News* Reference Library; Mark Harvey, photo archivist at the State Archives of Michigan; Thomas Featherstone of the Walter Reuther Library, Wayne State University; Sharon Brown of the Michigan State Police Central Records Division; John Currie and Mary Zumeth of the State Archives of Michigan; Penelope A. Morris, owner of the P. A. Morris Co., for her help in editing and creating a hard copy of the work; Walter Wasacz of the *Hamtramck Citizen* newspaper; and Officer Merle Van Marter.

For their support and encouragement, I would like to thank Rosalyn and Rick Smith; Georgia E. Wilder; Pat Henahan; my friends and colleagues at the Wayne State University Engineering Unit; and Mike Webb. A special thanks to Allan Wilson, Senior Editor, and Jeff Nordstedt, Vice President, Barricade Books; and to Carole and Lyle Stuart, Publishers, for having continued faith in my work.